C000121030

The Miracle of
HOSPITALITY

The Miracle of
HOSPITALITY

LUIGI GIUSSANI

Introduction by JULIÁN CARRÓN

Translated by MATTHEW HENRY

THE MIRACLE OF HOSPITALITY

Slant Books
P.O. Box 60295
Seattle, WA 98160

www.slantbooks.com

Cataloguing-in-Publication data:

Names: Giussani, Luigi.

Title: The miracle of hospitality.

Description: Seattle, WA: Slant Books, 2023.

Identifiers: ISBN 978-1-63982-130-3 (hardcover) | ISBN 978-1-63982-129-7 (paperback) | ISBN 978-1-63982-131-0 (ebook)

Subjects: LCSH: Giussani, Luigi. | Hospitality | Hospitality in the Bible | Hospitality--Religious aspects--Christianity.

All Bible quotations are taken from the Revised Standard Version, Catholic Edition.

Contents

Do not neglect to show hospitality to strangers,
for thereby some have entertained angels unawares.

—HEBREWS 13:2

Introduction

JULIÁN CARRÓN

WHY IS HOSPITALITY a miracle? It seems like something we should take for granted—opening the door of our home and letting someone in should be normal.

Why, then, does Father Giussani compare this to a miracle? Precisely because it should be the normal experience of every family, and yet it is so exceptional that when it happens everyone is amazed.

We live in a human, cultural, and social context that is the fruit of a long history, one that has witnessed the erosion of our awareness of elementary experience: in particular, the original openness of heart and the perception of reality as positive, as full of promise for our life. In time, things and people became extraneous to us—a distance was introduced. Jean-Paul Sartre's statement is terrible: "My hands, what are my hands? They are the incommensurable distance that divides me from the world of objects and separates me from them forever."[1]

As Pope Benedict XVI reminded the couples he met with in Ancona in 2011:

> In the confusion everyone is urged to act in an individual, autonomous manner, often solely on the perimeter of the present. The fragmentation of the community fabric

is reflected in a relativism that corrodes essential values;
the harmony of feelings, of spiritual states and emotions,
seems more important than sharing a plan for life. Even
basic decisions then become fragile, exposed as they are
to the possibility of revocation that is often considered
an expression of freedom, whereas in fact it points to the
lack of it.[2]

Precisely in this context, a family that opens its home to a child
or a person in difficulty—as the Italian organization Famiglie per
l'Accoglienza[3] does—expanding the horizon of their affections to
a "stranger," has in itself something of the divine that conquers
this distance. Father Giussani compares this welcoming to a passage from the Letter to the Hebrews: "Do not neglect to show
hospitality to strangers, for thereby some have entertained angels
unawares" (Hebrews 13:2). And he comments: "They are not just
angels: they are more than angels! They are children of God, part
of the mystery of the person of Christ. . . . It is like seeing one who
goes around by night completely fluorescent. And the people are
encouraged . . . seeing and reading what you are living."[4]

Here we see the importance of that original openness of heart
that faith reveals in its profundity, which makes an experience possible that would otherwise be unrealizable, especially in an epoch
like ours. The promise, in fact, is that the distance described by
Sartre can be overcome. And this helps us to understand that an
association like Welcoming Families is not the fruit of human
imagination—because that distance is unbridgeable for those with
limited resources, however generously they may be engaged. It is
another type of belonging, more a passivity than an initiative, as
Father Giussani says: "We cannot share, which means we cannot
put forward our presence as part of the presence of an other, we
cannot open our presence to welcome the presence of an other,
if first of all we do not feel ourselves welcomed, if we do not feel
ourselves loved."[5]

As Benedict XVI told the couples at Ancona: "You may be
certain that in every circumstance you are cherished and protected
by the love of God, who is our strength."[6] It is only this profound

amazement for something that happens in our life that becomes a condition for us to welcome the other, in imitation of Christ who called everyone "friend," even Judas the night of the ultimate betrayal, overcoming every distance. It is that profound sympathy which makes Jesus say to Zacchaeus, "Make haste and come down; for I must stay at your house today" (Luke 19:5). And that infamous man runs home and prepares everything for the unforeseen guest who will revolutionize his life.

Hospitality is the imitation of Christ's gesture. Every other reason would be either sterile sentimentalism or voluntarism—which the very first difficulties to arise would bring to its knees.

Those who share the gaze with which Christ looks at people and things can enter into the arena, accepting even difficult sacrifices, as inevitably happens to so many who share the life of children. This is a witness to the nature of Christianity: it does not require any titanic force or any particular capacity, because it breaks into life as something unforeseen that enters the "I" and changes it.

It is a thrilling experience to be invited to lunch by a family and see Christ at work while you are at table, through the signs of a humanity that treats everything in a new way, that is not reductionistic, with a charity and a patience that are impossible for humankind on our own. And then there is a joy, even within the difficulties and the everyday misunderstandings, that is already the victory over nothingness and over the banality into which our relationships can fall. "Concretely, there exists no act greater than hospitality: from a radical hospitality, like adoption, to a simple one like offering lunch or shelter to someone passing through town for a night. One of the most beautiful things I see happening among my friends is this connection, this network of families, open to accommodating anyone,"[7] Father Giussani recalled in 1985.

His dialogues with the Welcoming Families Association are a gift of the Mystery, that shows us a heart that is certain and for this reason capable of embracing anyone, making it easy to see how the memory of Christ is the root of every movement of the "I."

Hospitality is without measure and without calculation. It is, in fact, the communication of a fullness that upholds our life, the fruit of the unforeseen hospitality we first received, as it was for the Virgin Mary—her "yes" to the announcement of the angel generated the greatest good that the world could desire. Having welcomed the preference of the Mystery in her life, not getting in the way at all, not even protesting about her limits and fragility—as can easily happen to so many of us in front of the choice of God—she became the mother of the Son of God, who for two thousand years has passed through history and reached each of us in the situation where we find ourselves. Will we also have the simplicity of Mary to make room for Him, welcoming Him in the womb of our life?

This is the greatness of the challenge that every family faces, the only challenge that lives up to the stature of our humanity. Father Giussani said: "I have this 'yes' and that's it.... It would cost nothing more for you than it costs for me.... To say 'yes' to Jesus ... because if I did not say 'yes' to Jesus, I would not be able to say 'yes' to the stars of the sky or the hairs of your head."[8]

This is the deepest reason to say yes to an unknown child who enters our house for a time that we do not determine, because everything is in the hands of God. But a month or a year doesn't matter: what matters is that each instant of our life together is full of that yes to Him who makes everything and, having made them, preserves them for eternity.

Is there anything more interesting for a man and a woman than this collaboration in the work of the Father, this work of overcoming the emptiness of the world with the strength of a presence? The former Archbishop of Milan Angelo Scola reminds us: "The family is the great path and the first 'school' of communion, whose law is the total gift of self. Christians, proposing this path in all its beauty, in spite of their fragility, attempt to witness to men and women of our time, whatever their worldview may be, that the objective desire for the infinite that is at the heart of every experience of love can truly be realized. The family conceived like this is a precious patrimony for the whole of society."[9]

The form of this collaboration in the work of the Father, then, is free from every preconceived scheme, as Father Giussani reminds us in this tremendous passage:

> Is being a father or a mother to throw a fetus out of the mother's womb? No! And if you welcome a fetus made by another woman for two months, four months, five months, and you educate him, you are the mother, in the physiological and in the ontological sense of the term! And if you do this even without actually having that child at home because your husband does not want to, or because you are afraid and you don't feel called to it, even if you pray to God, in so far as you know a poor child in trouble, mistreated by a family that is not his, and you offer your whole day in the morning saying: "Lord, I offer you my day so that you may help this child," this is an even finer form of motherhood, more "genetic" than any other maternity. In fact, our mothers, who were Christian mothers, took care of us children like this![10]

Let us pray that a portion of this gaze may also become ours, that we may be protagonists in the daily struggle to affirm the inexorable positivity of reality in front of the nothingness that encroaches on our days, signaling the beginning of a new humanity.

Dear Friends,

YOUR EXAMPLE SHEDS A LIGHT for me on our future path: a familiarity—or fraternity—that opens itself up to embrace another without any hesitation. I urge you never to stop welcoming people in imitation of Christ who embraced the children He encountered.

If He, our Lord, offered young children as an example marking the way for adults, those of you who do the same thing He did are made signs of something new. This newness, like a wave, will spread from the nearest family to the farthest one, in a movement that is the beginning of a more human society, made of people who are passionate about human destiny. You would give your life for any one of them because you have met the One who gives life and breath to everything.

I pray that, by meeting you, people may finally feel at home, feel welcomed and safe like children in their father's arms.

Luigi Giussani
Letter to the Welcoming Families Association

The Reason for Charity

SHARING LIFE IN A HUMAN and Christian way does not require that the conditions of this act be conscious. Most of the time, they live implicitly in our good will—a will that is sustained, especially in difficult moments, by a reasoned explanation.

Therefore, when the Gospel says, "Take heed, watch and pray; for you do not know when the time will come" (Mark 13:33), it means: be conscious of your destiny, of your relationship with God, with the source, the substance, and the end of what you are.

This is the most important premise we must always remember.

I wanted to communicate the value of the implicit and of the unknown to you, because the gift of the Spirit and the grace of God can act within anyone; the Lord is not limited by anything. I also wanted to point out the importance of being vigilant, because the clarity, joy, and peace that come from an act of charity with well-defined aims are unparalleled. I hope to make a small contribution to the clarification of these aims.

If we want to feel ourselves immediately filled with richness in our thoughts, we must always start from this great, primordial truth: that we did not exist and now we do. Therefore, being—living, existing, moving—is participation in something else. How much peace there is in being able to say with clarity (with clarity regarding motivation, not regarding content, which is the mystery that Christ has revealed to us) that everything we do participates in something else! Here are the roots of gratuitousness (*gratuità*)[11]: everything we do and everything we are are given—we participate in something else. I believe that there is nothing more evident than this: that in every instant of our life we do not make ourselves. It is in the vibration of this self-awareness that the possibility of real prayer develops within us.

The root of gratuitousness is all here, precisely because nothing is ours. At the base, I am alluding to what the first page of the Bible says: "Let us make man in our image, after our likeness" (Genesis 1:26). This means that the life of the Mystery vibrates and echoes within humanity's dynamism, according to an immensely distant, yet real analogy. We can draw three conclusions from this.

The Awareness of Being Loved

If we do not feel welcomed or loved in the first place, we cannot share anything. In other words, we cannot make our presence part of another's presence—we cannot open our presence to welcome the presence of an other.

Here we understand that without God we face our problems without an adequate hypothesis. Because there can be generosity, openness, obedience, a great capacity for "hospitality" (to use a synthesizing word), even if we do not experience a human correspondence in any sense, but we have a clear perception of what is at the origin of this moment: if we live, it is because we are wanted, and if we exist, it is because we are loved.

I said a clear perception, but it could also be an unclear and confused awareness, a hunch or intuition, even in one who would not consider himself religious but who, without knowing it, really is. Whatever the case, without the presence of God on the horizon of our life, we cannot open ourselves in welcome, we cannot dedicate ourselves to sharing, nor can we accept a presence that is not our own and that, precisely because it is not ours, does not coincide with us.

Our behavior is defined by this imitation ("Let us make mankind in our image, in our likeness") or, like I said, by our participation in something else. For this reason, true religiosity is expressed in the ability to share and to welcome, before anything else and, in a certain sense, before even saying "God." If we have these things inside of us, it is because we already perceive God, however unconsciously.

In any case, only if we are loved can we love: loved not by the person and in the ways that we may desire, but in a way that is much deeper and more essential. I have understood this in experience. If a child is truly loved by his parents, he knows what love is, he grows up knowing it, even if he is unaware of this knowledge, even if this wisdom (yes, it is a real wisdom) is not reflected by him.

Forgiving Difference

The attitude of hospitality means the forgiveness of difference, which is defined by the Christian word "mercy."

To better understand the foundations and the motivation for hospitality, we shouldn't first think of the homeless that we welcome into our house, but of a wife, a husband, or a son as he grows up. If these factors do not emerge in our relationship with them, we are living these relationships blindly; we take them for granted; we are unaware of what is going on.

The word "mercy" indicates welcoming as an energy and a freedom that—like intelligence and affection—overcome the emptiness, the gap, the distance between differences. How amazing it is to think of the infinite distance which God overcame compared to our nothingness. The Bible says: "The Lord appeared to him from afar. I have loved you with an everlasting love; therefore I have continued my faithfulness to you" (Jeremiah 31:3). There is no greater difference than the distance between being and nothingness!

I believe this is an aspect of awareness that needs to be constantly revived in us. If a man welcomes a woman, paradoxically recognizing their difference *and* embracing her with this awareness, he will never embrace her more fully—he must be aware of this difference and embrace her in this awareness. I am not defining the mercy with which Christ shows us the living God, giving the last word on the living God, but I am emphasizing the striking connection that we are called to live with this mercy, because, as Saint Paul says, "But God shows his love for us in that while we were yet sinners Christ died for us" (Romans 5:8). If He loves us as sinners, imagine how much He must love us when we seek Him out and call on Him!

Love for the Person

Welcoming and sharing are the only ways to achieve a relationship that is worthy of our humanity, because only in this way is a person really a person, someone who exists in relationship with the Infinite. When speaking of children, Jesus said, "I tell you that in heaven their angels always behold the face of my Father who is in heaven" (Matthew 18:10). The path through which this sharing occurs—that is, the welcoming embrace of one presence to another presence—can take any form. Therefore, it can be any path so long as it has a point *a quo* [from which] and a point *ad quem* [to which]. The starting point [*a quo*] can be anything, even a trivial and concrete interest. But the point of arrival [*ad quem*] is always the person, a being whose angel sees the face of the Father, a being that is a relationship with the Infinite. My embrace of another cannot, then, be exhausted in the reasons for which I initially connected the other to me and accepted him. For this reason, welcoming a poor stranger and welcoming the person we love the most must ultimately be lived with the same gratuitousness, otherwise what should be the greatest thing sadly becomes obtuse and dull.

Participating in the initial Event, therefore, is the source of gratuitousness: within this event, our vigilance and awareness contribute to bringing a clarity and joy which would otherwise be more difficult to achieve.

Only if we are aware that we are loved—with clarity or confusion, implicitly or explicitly—can we love, which means to embrace, to welcome within us, and to share.

The great road we must take to make ourselves similar to the Bible's image of Christ—who comes to us from eternity, walking among us like a giant on our earth—is in overcoming difference:

mercy. Embracing another means embracing somebody different, remembering that God is the different, the ultimate other.

This itinerary of mercy can start from any cue, even the most trivial (the Lord is a master in this through nature), but it must reach a love for the presence understood as a place of relationship with the Eternal, with the Infinite. The point of arrival is the person who has an infinite destiny, who is a relationship with the Infinite.

Methodological Factors

1. Without *freedom*, there can be no welcoming, but only an illusory invitation—without freedom, the other would feel trapped, used, and exploited. Being fully oneself is what it means to be free. Freedom, therefore, is a necessary condition for the method of welcoming.

This freedom, which I defined as being fully oneself, has precise components. First of all, it regards the awareness of one's belonging to the Infinite, to the Mystery. The more a person lives his relationship with God, the more he is aware of and recognizes his destiny, and the more he has an affection for being. This affection for destiny and being, then, manifests itself in the peaceful affection for one's circumstances (which applies to all possible personalities: both a restless personality and a tranquil one will show this affection the best they can!).

Freedom, whose highest point is forgiveness for oneself, is the most difficult imitation of God: forgiveness is His "condemnation," mercy His way of judging. The humility which allows gratuitousness is rooted here, because humility comes from the awareness of our own misery, which vibrates, paradoxically, in a total certainty, because Christ is Risen, has won, and wins me.

2. The second methodological factor is what the Church Fathers stressed most when explaining Christ's relationship with man: His accommodation (His taking human flesh to shape Himself to meet our needs).[12] This freedom, this being oneself, must bend and

be molded, shaping Himself to the welcomed presence—to all the nooks and crannies, all the forms that presence may take.

This means that we must avoid pretension. We do not have any reason to expect the other to be different—that would not be welcoming! The desire that the other become himself, according to the ideal that our consciousness has of the relationship with God and the Infinite, is very different from any pretension. It is the desire to walk together toward the same destiny, Christ.

The realism of the condition on which our acceptance of another is founded is already implied in what we have called our itinerary and in what we have said about freedom. Accommodation as such insists on adapting to the other without having to make pretentious claims.

3. This *accommodation* is a *love of suffering*, not in a masochistic sense, but like Christ, who said, "My Father, if it be possible, let this cup pass from me" (Matthew 26:39). Suffering is born from the impossibility of a correspondence between the attitude or disposition of another and what we think or imagine, whether it is a good project for him or the satisfaction of our own need for affection. Pain is born when we realize that we are unable to fill the void of difference, because difference is truly an abyss that only a connection with the Infinite, with God, can overcome (think about husbands and wives, think of their differences when dealing with details; even that is an abyss!).

Gratuitousness, in practice, springs from this suffering. It purifies us deep down from our innate tendency to plan, our natural need for requited affection, and our natural propensity to manipulate. I am not saying that gratuitousness is the same thing as this suffering, but that suffering challenges us and purifies us, making our gratuitousness exist concretely. The purity of our gratuitousness is truly saved by suffering, by understanding suffering as a lack of correspondence that is at the root of almost every relationship, because only in the Eternal do we find true correspondence.

I always told my students a story which took place in the early years of my priesthood, which really moved me. A woman had been coming to me for Confession every week, when suddenly, she stopped coming. After a couple of months, she came back and told me she had given birth to her second daughter. She said, "You know, the first feeling I had when she was born was not curiosity as to whether she was a boy or a girl, or if she was doing well, but I thought, 'She is already beginning to leave!'" Accepting this separation is sublime gratuitousness. And this is the beginning of what every parent must face when it comes to their child's vocation. "Beginning to leave" means that when a child is born, she is born for her own destiny, one that the parents cannot determine, because vocation is given by God and no one else.

In the thirteenth chapter of Hebrews, Saint Paul says, "Remember those who are in prison, as though in prison with them; and those who are ill-treated, since you also are in the body" (Hebrews 13:3). When I read this passage, I am terrified, and I'd like to disappear, because I have participated, with all my freedom and conscience, in this Western Christianity that for fifty years did not once mention our brothers in Eastern Europe who are persecuted under the Soviet regime. Thank God that He has shaken us up with this Pope![13]

The verse from Saint Paul means that welcoming is empathy: you are me, and I am you. Hospitality is great if one understands and feels that every relationship is hospitality, welcoming another. But the word "hospitality" significantly expresses the entire phenomenon of welcoming. In that chapter, Saint Paul says, "Do not neglect to do good and to share what you have, for such sacrifices are pleasing to God" (Hebrews 13:16). Hospitality, in the strict sense of the word, is an empathy that operates according to all the concrete circumstances it faces. Concretely, there exists no act greater than hospitality: from a radical hospitality, like adoption, to a simple one, like offering lunch or shelter to someone passing through town for a night.

One of the most beautiful things I see happening among my friends is this connection, this network of families, open to accommodating anyone.

Living Gratuitousness

IT'S SO STRIKING—just imagine how it was for those who heard it directly—to hear Jesus say: "Apart from me you can do nothing" (John 15:5). As a seminarian, I was moved by a preacher who said, "Guys, this is not just a way of speaking." Many years later, I realized just how much we need to remember that it is indeed not just a way of speaking.

"Apart from me you can do nothing." And so, paradoxically, a great certainty of spirit and a great affection are born within us, like the child in his mother's arms (this is the constant comparison used by Jesus Himself). If we do not become like children, we will grow presumptuous, we will judge others, and we will build nothing, not even—in the microscopic space of our short lives—our "I."

Therefore, in his letter *Itinerari educativi* [Educational Itineraries],[14] Cardinal Martini said that the active subject and promoter of humanity's great educational project is the mystery of the Trinity. As we have said before, we are here as human beings, therefore as people journeying toward our destinies, and the active subject and promoter of this journey is not me but something I must welcome within me: the Holy Spirit, the mystery of the triune God. Beginning Day[15] must make us "lift our gaze," as the first great prophets often repeated (cf. Hosea 11:7). "Lifting our gaze" means entering into the great memory of Christ with all of our heart and soul. It is therefore a moment of enthusiasm for Christ and the mission He entrusts to us. In fact, this is the ultimate contradiction: we don't know how to do anything, yet He entrusts us with a mission (it isn't a contradiction, it's a paradox). Therefore, the memory of Christ and enthusiasm for the mission to which He has destined us are the two most important things: there is no one among us who is not destined to this mission, by the very fact that we all have heard the word "Jesus."

In his *A Short Story of the Anti-Christ*, Soloviev writes:

> Now, in a grieved voice, the Emperor addressed them: "What else can I do for you, you strange people? What do you want from me? I cannot understand. Tell me yourselves, you Christians, deserted by the majority of your peers and leaders, condemned by popular sentiment. What is it that you value most in Christianity?" At this, Elder John rose up like a white candle and answered quietly: "Great sovereign! What we value most in Christianity is Christ himself—in his person. All comes from him, for we know that in him dwells all fullness of the Godhead bodily."[16]

This is memory and mission. What comes from Him, from Christ who is the way in which the Mystery has entered our life and is dragging, pushing, guiding us toward our destiny? Everything! "Apart from me you can do nothing." If only this thought accompanied us more often throughout the year. If only we would remind each other of this! "That which we hold most dear in Christianity is Christ Himself. What we value most in Christianity is Christ himself—in his person. All comes from Him, for we know that in Him dwells all fullness of the Godhead bodily."[17]

I just reread what will now be the permanent manifesto of our movement:[18] there is no literary text that can better express the feeling that animates us. The great Lithuanian poet Czeslaw Milosz, recipient of the Nobel Prize in 1980, was invited by our friends to attend a public meeting in Italy at the San Carlo Cultural Center. After seeing this manifesto, he exclaimed: "What? You say these things? Now I know I can trust you people!" When I heard about this, I thought to myself: how many of us still find it hard to trust, after all we have received! However, this is the mission: to make Christ known, because Christ is the Salvation of man. Christ is the Redeemer of man. This year we will celebrate the tenth anniversary of the encyclical *Redemptor Hominis*.[19] The whole of our Pope's prophetic inspiration, the force of his love and passion for Christ and for people, is in the title of his first encyclical: "Christ, the Redeemer of Man." Without Christ, human beings are not themselves, do not know themselves, and do not reach fulfillment. The great evangelization that the Pope always talks about—that all may recognize and love Christ the redeemer of man—is entrusted to us, our hands, and our hearts. So, let us lift our gaze at the beginning of this new stretch of our lives, a long stretch of a short life ("threescore and ten, or even by reason of strength fourscore," Psalm 90:10).

The Concreteness of a Story

As the first point, I would like us to remember one important thing: relationships with Christ—*my* relationship with Christ—can only pass through the concreteness of a story within which He persuasively and pedagogically shows Himself to me, evoking a creative capacity within me. Without obeying or adhering to the concrete historical way through which we have had the encounter—and I mean without passing through historical, concrete ways through which Christ made Himself known to us in a persuasive way, even if it was only a moment (we have understood that the faith can be persuasive for our reason, our heart, and useful for our life and the life of all people)—if, in short, we do not live in relationship with the concrete way through which Christ came toward us and engaged our humanity, if we do not respect the love of and attachment to what we call "movement"—without this historical depth, we pursue our own image of Christ, just as we can pursue our own image of the movement.

In front of the world, in front of our worldly context, we need to be determined by something that precedes the world. This worldly context is concrete: think of the television and the magazines, how everyone—everyone!—is assailed, is invaded by them, and therefore everyone repeats what the television and the mass media feed them. In front of this concrete world, we must be determined by a concrete origin, which means the building up of our friendship and of our movement. This gives depth to our presence. The more we belong to this reality which was born through the Holy Spirit, by the grace of an encounter, the more our presence makes a difference, proposes itself and opens itself to everything and everyone, because knowing Christ means suddenly feeling that the world is part of my being and my heart.

In his pastoral plan, Cardinal Martini reminds us that within the global Christian itinerary there is room for "many personal and communitarian paths, within which the journey of this immense people of God is articulated."[20] Our companionship is a way in which the journey of this immense people of God is articulated. We did not choose it. We have not chosen it. If we are here, it is because we were moved by something. It is God who makes it, the Lord who chooses, elects, and commands. This initiative of God creates in us a capacity, sensitivity, and desire to communicate that which was previously unknown to us, and, therefore, through our adherence to His choice, He creates a companionship that, when expanded, can be called a movement. It is only within the concrete reality of a companionship, of a movement, that one can face the world. One could follow the path of a hermit, which would be an exceptional case, but usually one's personal itinerary tends to generate companionship and movement.

Therefore, when we lift our gaze in this memory of Christ (as Dionysius the Areopagite said, "Christ, if I may say so, you are 'mine'"), herein lies the enthusiasm for the mission that we were handed, whoever and wherever I may be, wherever and however I will be tomorrow. (This morning in bed, when I woke up very early, I thought, "What if I had to stay here and could no longer move?" I understood that this thought would be my only salvation, because "the glory of the king's daughter" (Psalm 45:14) is in the awareness with which I recognize You, O Lord, and love You despite what I am. Therefore, there is only one sin that cannot be forgiven: the refusal of the urgency with which Christ bangs on our half-open door—or closed door, even—assailing it and begging at it, *dives in misericordia*, rich in mercy.) Raising our gaze in this memory and with enthusiasm, I was saying, we must pay a first tribute of awe, gratitude, and intelligent love to the life of our companionship, to the life of our movement. Certainly, a small group may be more needy or richer than another. Some may seem to be more fortunate, but through all the concrete facts of our daily life, Christ guides us on our journey ("I am the way, and the truth, and the life," John 14:6).

Gratuitousness

Given the necessity to lift our gaze, the second word I want to emphasize is the one that best characterizes the way the Mystery communicates Himself, the one that exemplifies Christ's reality among us, the Mystery among us. This word is *gratuitousness* (there is no stronger or more powerful word than this, and we cannot express ourselves in any other way). Gratuitousness is love without profit, without human motives, without reasons that reason can understand or explain, without the obligation to adhere or to obey.

He came *gratis*, in this *caritas*, in this charity. "Why did you create me?" "Because I loved you!" "And why did you love me?" "Because I loved you!" "And why did you come, in the confusion and darkness of the world, as light on my journey, on my road, taking hold of me, and placing me within You, within the Mystery of Your person, and calling me to communion with You?" "Because I loved you!" "And why did you love me?" "Because I loved you!"

Gratuitousness is the infinite, which is a reason in and of itself. "And in the long story of the Christian people, so easily distracted, so easily deterred from its center by the world in which we live, so easily abandoned like sheep abandoned by its shepherds, why did you come to me so concretely, on a specific occasion that provoked in me a different attitude and different way of life?" "For love, for charity, *gratis*, freely."

So, when we start meditating on the fact that what is dearest in Christianity is Christ Himself, we cannot help but desire—trembling, perhaps, but desiring with our whole heart—to imitate Him, to follow Him into this astonishing thing that leaves us speechless: the fact that He loved us gratuitously. We cannot avoid desiring to follow Him in this charity (*charis*, gratuitousness).

This year we want to help each other more, so that our spirit may be more united to His. At the beginning (let's try to imagine those first months), the apostles followed Him and were filled with admiration and affection, attached but unable to desire being like Him because this desire burst open only when the Spirit of Christ descended upon them on Pentecost. Then they understood! How often He repeated in His long speech before His death, "You do not fully understand yet, you cannot understand, but I will send the Spirit." Now, this Spirit has descended on us all. The Spirit descends on us every day, because He has called us to be filled by It. So this year we must make the imitation of His charity our main theme. It must be the main passion in our relationship with Christ and therefore the most cherished aspect of our companionship.

The truest work in our life is that work which is unpaid, the work of a change of ourselves and, through ourselves, the work of changing the world. This change in us—and through us—is our way of collaborating in the transfiguration of the cosmos and of history that the Pope always talks about: it is true participation in the *opus dei*, the work of the mystery of the Trinity in the world, the work of Christ in the world. Gratuitousness means facing our relationship with ourselves, and with everything else, in the light of destiny and because destiny became man, in the light of Christ and the perspective of Christ. Rest assured, when this happens, people and things do not fall into monotony and become pretenses. When seen with the eyes of Christ, in the light of Christ, people become more themselves, and things, too, if held in the same love with which Christ loved us, become more themselves.

Earlier I used the word "work" because it encompasses the totality of our day (work is not just eight hours in the office or the factory). Gratuitousness must become the soul of our work. Even atheists can sense it: Cesare Pavese said that to carry pain without finding an adequate meaning for it is unbearable and ignoble.[21] But the adequate meaning of the difficulty inherent in work, and of the suffering that always accompanies our work and relationships, the one who gives us a reason to persevere, is Christ, destiny made man.

There is something that must truly change in our way of facing daily life. A certain nobility, which is largely unknown to us, of which we feel the need, must become habitual, so that life can become dignified, full of fascination and gusto. We need the experience of gratuitousness. It was this idea that created the *Compagnia delle Opere*.[22] The idea that we must learn how to face our work turned toward the ultimate meaning of ourselves, the ultimate meaning of each person's story, that is Christ. Consequently, all the effort we put into our work should reverberate with attention and tenderness toward others, like children or the sick who, like us, need to be taken by the hand and helped to walk. This is what allows people to move, and nothing less.

At this point, I wish I could read the many witnesses (I brought them with me) that the Welcoming Families Association sent me. The work of Welcoming Families is not something "peculiar": it is a great inspiration that is leavening all the communities of the movement. May Christ help us and may Our Lady, in her month of October, expand this generosity and its possibilities!

I'm sorry that I cannot read them right now, but I will quote some passages. "Through the failing of some relationships [her husband left her, and her mother died], I understood that I was in this world for Christ." This is exactly what they all say in one way or another. All the families that welcome and live this hospitality are not responding to an invitation to collaborate with public entities in meeting some need or other but are responding to a passion for something greater, for a meaning that lives as an expectation in their hearts, for the meaning of their lives. All the members of Welcoming Families, in one way or another, repeat this in the letters they send me (for which I am grateful): "In our difficulties, we understood that we are in the world for Christ," meaning for the Redeemer of man, for the salvation of man, for He who is the salvation of man. If we came into the world for Him who is the salvation of man, then our whole life—even the narrowness with which we sometimes perceive it—cannot avoid desiring to do some good to others and to participate in the difficulties of another's journey.

"When we met the community and the movement ten years ago, we were an empty family, although nothing seemed to be missing. At that time, we had a son. The absence of meaning in our life had isolated us. We were giving in to the anguish of loneliness. This surprising and unexpected encounter reawakened a gusto for life, giving us energy and vitality that we had never experienced before. Feeling welcomed without any demands by our friends from Welcoming Families seemed to us to be the way we could give back to others and help them find purpose in their lives again. Our house became open to the needy. First, baby Mario came to us for a couple of months. Then three brothers came for a longer period. We welcomed them simply, offering them our house and what we had. I remember that in difficult moments, and they weren't few, we would pray to the Lord to help us. We did not even have cots to put on the ground. Then Nella, an alcoholic, came and Pietro, a drug addict, and these experiences were filled with suffering. Nella died after her time with us, and Pietro, after being completely clean for the four years he spent with us, relapsed."

There is another example, a shockingly beautiful one, that I hope you will read in *Litterae Communionis*.[23] It is a letter from our friend Rose, recounting an episode at the end of a shift at the hospital where she works (she is a nurse), when she saw a leper dragging himself on his four stumps. He had traveled one kilometer in three hours to seek treatment at the hospital. He had dysentery, and no one wanted to touch him. You can read how she welcomed him.[24]

However, we must keep one thing in mind with regard to charity. Our community is filled with these examples, and one would like to quote them one after the other. (I should quote one after the other of the ones I know—there are hundreds! Like how one of you who lost her husband and welcomed a woman sick with terminal AIDS into her home. After six months, the woman passed away in peace and happy because of the companionship she had been offered.)

In front of these great examples of charity that fill the life of our community (it makes me want to talk only about these stories), especially in front of the example of the Welcoming Families (hospitality is the most difficult form of charity; it engages you completely, from morning to night and from night to morning, like a son, a brother, or a husband), I want to make an observation: all of this must become a struggle that changes us from within. After seeing our brothers and sisters, our friends, our companions, and the families that are with us perform this gratuitous hospitality, we can no longer be as we were before. We may tremble and feel incapable of this, because the Spirit is handed out according to the measure of Christ, but the Spirit is given so that even we may change: "If another can give a hundred, Lord, I can at least offer you one."

It is a struggle that pushes us to change ourselves. We should not praise these families from afar. We must not look at these things behind our walls of self-sufficiency, benevolently or admiringly. We find ourselves stopping at mere admiration—but no, these things must *define* us. This is not about being touched, but about being shocked and changed. In fact, the generosity of Welcoming Families raises the bar for the whole community.

Belonging, Source of the Criterion

There is a third and final thing I want to touch on. There is no authentic gratuitousness if we do not live with gratitude for the charity with which Christ has touched our lives through the lives of others, the encounter with a companionship. Without faithfulness to the companionship that we have met, our charity would be false. It would not make history—that is, it would not truly contribute as it should to the Kingdom of God and to the building up of the Kingdom of God.

Here's an example. One of you wrote to me: "When the media began to say certain things about the Meeting in Rimini, I asked myself, 'What's going on?' So, I decided to immerse myself in a place that expresses my identity and went to the Meeting.[25] I understood, and I came back peaceful." What you did and said are correct, my friend.

Now, let us imagine a large community in which only three people went to the Meeting. Everyone was speechless whenever one of these three spoke about what happened at the Meeting, but they were also full of objections, the same objections that we hear on TV and read in the press. But when you make these objections your own, you are actually living out of a belonging—you belong to the world of TV and the press. Instead of starting from the same experience, like the first man did ("I decided to take a dive"), you allow your opinion to prevail and you distance yourself from what your companions in the movement are doing. You are not even close to noticing that your opinion is influenced by the dominant mentality, the mentality of power.

In every sphere this is how it goes: either the origin, the root, determines your concern, your belonging—the companionship to which you belong, to which Christ makes you belong—or, while claiming to affirm your own opinions and judgments, you are hindered by and confined inside the great prison that worldly power is constructing around you.

Many years ago, Bishop Bartoletti, then Secretary of the Italian Conference of Bishops, asked some of us who were visiting him, "Where is your Statute?" They responded, "We do not have a Statute." "But how can you be so cohesive, so united, without a Statute?" In the end, he himself concluded, saying, "I understand. Your friendship is your Statute." I do not know if he really understood the depth of the word he used, the deep well of faith and charity that constitutes the human reality of our friendship, but this is true.

An example along these lines is given to us by an engineer and CEO of a large company. While asking to join the School of Community and the movement, he wrote:

> Reading the polemic in *Il Sabato*[26] on common values opened up a question for me: What is Christianity? After

I met you all, I felt pain and bitterness for how I had lived my life in such a way that, in the name of a generic dedication to Christian ideals, I had excluded Christ. The newspapers won't ever report that Communion and Liberation, as I now understand it, is a movement for the holiness of the person, that it has the courage to bet everything on this desire. What shocks me about your political relationships is that the criterion is not political. In politics, in fact, we can agree with anyone without ever having an identity. In front of your proposal, though, everyone must respond by name and not by whatever label he or she may have. I was taught that life was a Mystery, but it was as if this lesson did not count. After I met you all, I cannot say exactly what the Mystery is, but I can say that I encountered it. I ask you to accept me into your community, because I do not want to lose this encounter. I would like to start doing an apostolate in my work environment, but I am so clumsy in starting that I ask myself, after thirty years of work, what I have learned to do, seeing that being a missionary is, in the end, the meaning of work. I believe that I must start again, from zero, and I need new teachers. At this point, it is not enough to have a career. I need to be convinced that the moments I value can last forever.[27]

The space between the initial perception that we had and the "forever" is this openness to learning.

Of course, we can have different reactions and thoughts regarding contingent things! What does this mean? It means that the same origin, the passion for the same origin, leads me to say something different than you, my friend. But I do this with respect for you, with desire to clarify my ideas for you, with tenacity in trying to correct what I think is your mistake, with patience in waiting for you, asking you for equal patience and tenacity toward me. Then our difference becomes something else; it is no longer about distancing yourself, but about entering more and more into everything! This is gratuitousness.

I wanted to mention that the most impressive aspect of gratuitousness is the life of our companionship, the life of the movement, because it is sewn together by one thing: Christ. The movement could not be held together—we cannot obey it, follow it, serve it, use it to serve—if not for the ultimate goal of our common destiny, which is Christ. Herein lies the enthusiasm we have for our movement, this is its only origin, and no one could leave and become better—no one! One could quote the dreadful phrase by Saint John, "They went out from us, but they were not of us" (1 John 2:19).

How was Christ's love given to us, the gratuitousness that marked the love of Christ for us? Christ loved us in obedience to the Father and adherence to the gratuitousness of the love of the Trinitarian mystery. But, as a man, it was because of this devotion to the mystery of the Father that He loved and chose us.

This is what we want to develop in this year, but in a dense way, in the density of concrete daily life, helping each other with mercy so that we may increasingly imitate this gratuitousness in our lives.

There is an infinity of examples among us that should make today different from yesterday and awaken in us a divine restlessness. We are not afraid of following. Let us remember that everything can happen, if we allow this first thing to happen: the grace that led me to meet you, friend, that allowed me to feel for one instant that my destiny was identical to yours, that instant in which we met, when we recognized each other, even without saying it or understanding it, and yet it so truly happened that we are here today!

Cardinal Martini, in his pastoral plan, tells us that the liturgy, the liturgical life, is an instrument to teach us this gratuitousness. Therefore, this year, we will try to develop our prayer following the sacramental life more intensely, humbly, and faithfully.

May the Eucharist bring an ever-greater visibility to our companionship and, therefore, of our communion, so that the Church, the whole Church, the Church in our country, and the Church throughout the whole world, may anticipate, always more visibly, the coming of Christ! This is, in fact, salvation. Salvation is His second coming, when He will come and reveal Himself. We get up every morning to anticipate, even in our poverty, His coming, His revelation.

"Our senses with thy light inflame, our hearts to heavenly love reclaim."[28] "Our senses with thy light inflame": may the meaning of the faces that we touch and the things that we use, Christ, in some way dictate even the way we embrace each other!

A New Experience of Humanity

THE FACT THAT THE WORK of Welcoming Families is within the history of the movement is clear from what we spoke about this morning. Welcoming Families is part of the history of the movement if its individual families are joined to the life of their community: it is enough that they are within the life of the movement, that they seek to live the life of the movement. You can live this life on the margins, without being aware of its developments, and thus the influence of its life on what you live will stop at a certain level; if instead you live the life of the community more and participate more in deepening your awareness within the movement, this will influence your way of understanding everything.

Your Association is a work of people, of persons. Thanks be to God, it was born from people of the movement. This has given the Association certain characteristics from the beginning, at least at the level of needs—because the individuals were within the life of the movement—that otherwise it would not have.

You have a great responsibility, because Welcoming Families is a work that should inspire the whole movement, all the families in the movement. In front of certain facts, we cannot stand by indifferently, either with an admiration from a distance or with a brief emotion that makes us go on as if nothing happened. Approaching certain experiences which other people have should be decisive for us: maybe someone will simply give a little more for the poor in the Common Fund! The more the individual members of Welcoming Families enter into the life of the movement and follow, the more they participate in the development of awareness within the movement, the more they will show a sensibility and a deeper desire, from our point of view, in asking questions and in their family life, in developing relationships with others in the Association and in proposing conversations.

We are "Welcoming Families" only because we grew up within the history of the movement; so even things that were not immediately comprehended were a means through which the Lord called us to deepen and verify the concreteness of what we heard. And even this is a blessing. To be helped in welcoming others means first of all to be built up in the experience of communion, in the family and beyond.

The vast majority would tend to separate you all, to label you as the "competent ones" because of an unconscious fear: "We are not able to be like they are." They don't feel up to being like that. They would be like the fox from Aesop because of this unconscious fear.

We experienced something that confronted us directly: seeing how certain families were already on the way, already mature and making progress. And, among the surprise and the joy at this, we said yes. It would be enough for many families to have a little push in order to make this step, a step that can help the couple and the children to mature. Lately, some families near us, who met the movement a few years ago, affirm that, thanks to this encounter, they have found joy and peace again and have even started welcoming others.

We must look, as this man has done, with prudence, if a family is in a favorable position to receive this invitation. It is better to exaggerate in excess than in deficiency. It is better to be indiscriminate in proposing rather than too timid, but we shouldn't make others feel guilty if they cannot help. Because this availability and this sensibility are a grace that God has given to you.

The Welcoming Families Association is a point of reference for the formation of many families who, through us, can discover that the generosity from which we began is the sign of something else. The movement has taught us that generosity on its own will fail: hope fades and we abandon the gesture, or we carry it forward with a moralistic effort. We, for now, offer the testimony of those who already live this experience and a network of friendship. More than this testimony and this companionship, we do not think of looking for anything else.

There is nothing more than this. The movement is an experience of faith, lived to the point of charity.

At the Fraternity vacation, there was a girl who suffered from AIDS; three or four families extended an offer of hospitality to her, after she was at a clinic for a year and a half, because no one wanted to face the problem. The people at the clinic were really struck. There is a great awareness in this regard. I think that, on the one hand, it doesn't have to do with asking for authorization: whoever feels up to getting in the game should get in the game; on the other hand, it is right that the one who guides the community uses these experiences as an example.

This is what we ask for from the Church of God and what we should ask for among ourselves. Can we not get something written down, a documentation, a significant example from your story? This is all very important for the task of education.

The relationship with people from the Association was the point of departure for a gratuitous companionship among people, on a common path toward our own destiny. It seems urgent to us, even within the community of the movement, to continue this patient work of companionship and of reciprocal accompaniment, of sharing in a path.

The only concern is that you, who are in the movement and feel this urgency, live more consciously in the movement. The rest will come. Even with the idea of fraternity,[29] we do not need to be artificial: you are already a fraternity. More a fraternity than anybody! With this beginning day, the Welcoming Families Association can become an example, a proposal for everyone. I am not saying that everyone can join the Welcoming Families, but this experience is the most exemplary fact from the point of view of the maturity of our lives: there is no fact more exemplary than this. What interests me is the story and a series of examples. The movement is not born from a discourse, but from an experience.

Someone told me about a woman who said she didn't feel Jesus Christ. But how does one feel Jesus Christ, how do we get to know Him and feel Him? When you change the way you act, the way you relate to others, because of the awareness of Christ. If you forgive someone who hurt you, you forgive because Christ says to forgive, then that experience of forgiveness is an experience of Christ. Because Christ is a human experience, which implies, for example, the capacity to forgive. The others don't know this; the one who has never really forgiven cannot understand what forgiveness is. It is analogous for you. The welcoming you do for people that are not of the same house or the same blood is like the experience of our Father in heaven: it is the experience of Christ.

For many of us, experiencing Christ through a stranger who enters our house has meant re-living and changing our relationship with our own children, with our husband or wife. The experience of welcome gives evidence of the centrality of Christ and meaning to our bonds of blood. I have experienced it this year, when they called me to work with families who were adopting. While never having had direct experience of adoption, in living the companionship with these families, I was helped to deepen my experience of maternity: I returned home and looked at my children in a different way; I couldn't be like I was before. It is true, Christ is an experience of what it means to be human!

You cannot enter into relationship with Christ if not through historical, concrete conditions, in which you are moved; otherwise, our thought about Christ is abstract. And this is something that is given.

I work in a neonatal unit, and for years I've found myself arguing every day about the problems of deformation, often fighting with colleagues and nurses for whom, when a deformed baby is born and brought to us, it is natural to say: "What is there to do? Let's hope he dies!" I found myself saying for years: "What kind of Christian are you, if you want their parents to have to suffer their whole life with a baby in this kind of situation?" I wanted to tell you about Daniele, the little baby in my unit whom we took home with us. It was an occasion that was not forced on us. It came to my wife's mind, who does not work in my unit and who saw this baby only once. She came home and said: "Why don't we take him?" It was not an instinctive decision: we let two and a half months go by from when she first said it. It was something alive and real. The story of Daniele really shook up my unit. Everyone asked themselves: "Why?" At the beginning, I defended myself, saying: "It was above all my wife who made the choice. I was more hesitant and afraid." But everyone let themselves be questioned: "We had him for five months in the unit, and we took care of him, but no one ever even thought of taking him home." And because everyone in the unit knows about my experience with Communion and Liberation, it was natural for them to connect this choice with the experience that I live. That baby could have remained there and then gone to a care facility, which would be the normal destiny, because no family would have adopted him. With the experience of welcoming, it is as if no one needs even to explain who Jesus Christ is; you see Him clearly in the gesture.

When I was a neuropsychiatrist for children in Reggio Emilia, a family had a child who up until then had not moved, did not grow, did not see, did not hear. The mother had felt and experienced that this baby could be a gift for her; she experienced that this young girl was a strong provocation for her life and loved her all the same. She wanted to know why: "Where is the origin, where did this affection take shape?" Welcoming Families, thanks to the movement, can be a help in understanding this origin.

The members of Welcoming Families are the most obvious example of what maturity looks like in our life. If a family welcomes a handicapped child, how could I not welcome my classmate, even if he smells?

For me, Welcoming Families was the manifestation of all that the movement has taught us about the topic of family.

The family is the keystone from which the whole bridge, the whole architecture of society, begins. Therefore, the well-being and the value of the family are simply the corollary of the vision we have of the whole. If you begin from families that have been destroyed—who do not have a vision of the whole—you cannot understand. Precisely because the family is the fundamental point of society, the well-being of the family derives from a healthy conception of society. Therefore, it is artificial to put the family in first place. Putting the study of the family in first place does not allow us to put the work of the whole in the foreground. And because the family is the keystone around which the whole is built, to understand the family, we need to understand the whole; if one does not understand the principle of the movement, the life of the Fraternity, the companionship, the companionship at work and at school, we cannot understand the family. When we begin to understand our companions at work, at school, etc., and we begin to "free ourselves" from the family, then the feeling is more powerful, and the family gives its reward.

Two years ago at Rimini, you said: "One feels called and turns her gaze." The experience of welcome, which the Association has been for me and my husband, is this continual feeling of being called. To welcome someone into our home, to have him there from morning to evening, is like hearing that same voice that says, "Turn around!" And while one turns around and looks, she also sees the reality of the history in which she is placed. The friendship with Welcoming Families has been an experience of conversion, within the movement, within the story of the people of God: He called me other than how I thought He would call me.

The problem of vocation is connected to this, not from the individual, but from the cultural point of view, such that one becomes a dialectical mirror for the other. For example, I say to the *Memores Domini*[30]: before welcoming someone into your house, you have to think about it thirty-four times; not for nothing are children given to parents who are male and female; you are not male and female; you should have the maturity of a sixty-year-old. A house of *Memores Domini* is a terrible place for welcoming, because the members have to welcome someone without the connection that is established in a family, the male/female connection.

Having to think again about how this capacity for welcoming others was generated, I realize that paradoxically it has not been the encounter with "welcoming" families: I learned hospitality from people who simply lived the experience of the movement. This is so true that the first step toward welcoming others, in the concrete and practical sense of the term, was a completely unconscious step, if I think about it now.

It is the sign of a vocation: those unconscious steps are the sign of a vocation. The vocation is given by God, whether we want it or not; while for our work, we need to use our inclination as a first criterion.

The very nature of this experience of welcoming others is not something that can be published. It demands discretion and provokes the dimension of freedom, which is an encounter among those who are waiting for it—

—and those who are already engaged. There are three movements of God toward man: first, election (God calls us to Himself); second, vocation (the content of this election); third, the command (the task which is entrusted to our vocation).

This morning, when you spoke about Welcoming Families, I thought that it could be taken as a command to be obeyed. On the other hand, this thought quickly vanished, because the experience of welcome is such that you can't go five minutes without getting to the heart of the question. And from this, one can also follow the indication that is given. I am in the Welcoming Families Association because I obeyed my wife who said: "Go!" And so, I'm here.

The true concept of obedience is not adhering to something without reason. Even if it is not conscious, reason is always implied, which does not mean adapting yourself to a model, but assuming a criterion and growing in affection for a history.

Now, I feel like I truly want to be open to the whole world. Monsignor Cox, in the first meetings we had in 1983, said that he had never seen an experience like the experience we were living. And so, at this point, I feel myself led to the movement within this obedience and openness—

—to go to the heart of the very experience of the movement, which by its nature cries out to the whole world. Others in the movement exchange this for the presumption of being the only good ones. That which is the fruit of a love is exchanged for a presumption.

In the encounter with the movement, my wife and I were "struck by lightning." This catapulted us into a new horizon. Within these solid roots of the movement, there is always a great appetite to continue on this journey, because it is an experience of love, an experience that launches us beyond our conceptions and our human abilities. Recently, before the vacation, we spent fifteen days in the mountains on retreat. After thirty-two years of marriage, it was the first time that we prayed so much to the Lord that He would illuminate the future of our family. We returned, and the Lord put us in front of very precise signs to which we could not say no, and we continue on this path of welcoming new people (five kids), that even goes against common sense. We are confident in the fact that the Fraternity has put us in motion.

It was in this Fraternity where you found an education, and thus a first expression of a reality that calls you and helps you to walk through everything.

Our experience began from a decision that some of us made with respect to a need that was put in front of us, the need of young mothers. The bishop called us, offered us an office, and asked us to begin this work. But this was possible thanks to the Welcoming Families Association. The person who is closest to us is the bishop, who encourages us to become ever more faithful in this work, so much so that recently he entrusted the diocesan clinic to us.

This is an engagement analogous to what the movement should be for you—not first of all a work, but a person. All this is a by-product of the essential experience that we call "movement."

The struggle of the movement today is often in the fact that everyone in the world around us agrees on the common values of life—except those in favor of abortion and euthanasia—everyone is moved by these human values. But even someone who is moved by these values and acts to support them will find that their actions fade away if the origin of their doing and their generosity is unclear—that is, if it is not centered on the fact of Christ.

The first fundamental question is not how to spread the movement, or to alleviate the needs of others, or the humanitarian emotion that we feel, but the recognition of and love for a new fact in the world and in history that represents the destiny of everything that is born. That is the essence of the experience of the movement. That is the problem. It is a personal problem, not a collective one. If one out of a hundred of us live it, this influences the hundred. If, among the hundred, ninety-nine are in CL and don't live this, they don't do anything good.

"Not of Flesh, Nor of Blood, but of God Are We Born"

I AM NOT A PART of the experience that those of you in Welcoming Families are called to live. Therefore, I do not know how pertinent my attempt at a response will be. I feel better answering your questions one by one. Often, when people who are getting ready to marry come to ask me what they should do, I say: "Come back later and tell me yourselves, because I am not called to live your vocation. I have to learn from you what I should say to others." Therefore, I am so thankful to you and the other authors for their testimonies. I will use your testimonies as much as possible to speak to you about what, from the human and Christian point of view, seems to constitute the greatest work, not only what our movement, but what a movement in general, can accomplish.

Recognizing the fact that unites us, our greatest human and Christian work is that the peculiarity and individuality of our family could open itself to the point of welcoming what, humanly speaking, seems strange—indeed, even strange and hostile, something really different from what we expect (which in fact we generally receive with a certain instinctive hostility).

I have often defined the experience of *forgiveness* as an experience of *welcoming what is different*. I say this initially for the husband and wife: without welcoming what is different—in short, without the experience of forgiveness—there cannot be a stable life together. The whole world gives witness to this. This is why Welcoming Families represents the greatest, most significant work.

The first characteristic of a Christian family is its capacity for hospitality (either welcoming a child for a time or adoption). The capacity of a Christian family—of any family—to recognize as its own child someone who doesn't have anything to do with their flesh and blood is precisely the fulfillment of the first chapter of the Gospel of Saint John: "who were born, not of blood nor of the will of the flesh nor of the will of man, but of God" (John 1:13). For this reason, even from the point of view of education, which is the call of the whole life of the community, Welcoming Families is the most explosive work!

I wanted first of all to underline what is most pressing for me. That which gives life to this work is impossible, humanly speaking (not for nothing is the indissolubility of marriage founded on the same basis as the call to virginity, that is, "for the sake of the kingdom of heaven," Matthew 19:12). Therefore, as a testimony, Welcoming Families in my opinion constitutes the most pedagogically remarkable work, the most important of all the works born from the movement.

Hospitality does not mean giving something—it means giving everything; it implies a whole life. To welcome another means to put our house, our time, and our energy at the disposal of another: the "I" becomes totally involved. This is charity in the fullest sense of the word, because reason recognizes the fact of Christ as an objective or a prophetic unity. It may even happen that a family is entrusted with children who are not Christian, and even there, it is for Christ that parents accept a Muslim child.

In the second place, the experience of Welcoming Families highlights (even if it is not a condition *sine qua non*) the difficulty of accepting a difference that is not easy to manage and demands a capacity for the sort of forgiveness, as I said before, that is so rare.

These are the first thoughts that always come to me when I think of Welcoming Families. Every time I speak, your Association is a privileged point of reference. Love for Christ is not something that *inspires* certain relationships, but something that *coincides* with those very relationships. And this makes us understand that love for Christ is not an emotion but a different way of treating man and nature. The love of Christ coincides with this. Sometimes I say to those who are getting ready for marriage: "The love of Christ coincides with the man-woman relationship so truly that we call it a sacrament, a reality that increases the fact of Christ in the world."

There are those who even take in six, seven, eight, nine, ten guests; while another family may not be able to do this. Therefore, we shouldn't measure: we should never measure—measuring is the negation of charity.

Now, since you have a communal life and a spirit of sacrifice, since you have a patient acceptance for the children you adopt, who are entrusted to you, by analogy the first environment where this welcoming should be imitated is among yourselves. First of all—paradoxically—between husband and wife. For example, a wife cannot accept a child in generosity if she is not sure that her husband will follow her in this—otherwise, this is destructive rather than constructive. But I do not want to enter into the particulars of family life now, even if that is something you should do.

The first community which this pedagogy should help is the community you have among yourselves—a help toward achieving a balance among you, a help so that all those who are engaged in this work may do so in a balanced way. I have already given a first example, anticipating what I wanted to say: balance is like health, the health of a moral and physiological equilibrium. You should help each other in this, because generosity can try to do everything, can stretch itself excessively, and then ungenerosity can "get back" at those who were open at first, in the form of pettiness. Therefore, this balance means to remind yourselves humbly of your limits and to remember the generosity with which you began.

But in this help toward balance there should be a hope, which might appear naïve or abstract: you are collaborating among yourselves, a collaboration among families who welcome others. If a family—everyone in agreement, balanced—gets itself into a certain condition, and something happens to throw it off balance, the first charity should be toward this family (in this sense it falls to you eventually to ask the Fraternity of the movement for help). The first sharing of need should be among families who are welcoming others, as a help toward an equilibrium that accepts your limits. We need to practice asking for help and sharing our needs.

In the third and last place, as in every work, we always need a point of reference. Therefore, I conceive this group of leaders as a point of reference for the whole work, which means having an eye toward the whole work. The observation of the whole work depends on you, to substitute provisionally what cannot otherwise be substituted, etc. For example, if something happens to a family, it can be fixed as soon as possible; so there needs to be an eye toward the whole situation, an immediate help. And here the word "balance" should govern everything.

A "nota bene." I see people here from other cities: I would recommend that, from the point of view of the movement, Welcoming Families be a work that includes the entire movement, so that, for example, even a family from Catanzaro in Southern Italy can have something to do with Welcoming Families, participate in their life, and on the other side, that the central nucleus of Welcoming Families can also be reminded of the family from Catanzaro.

In what way does the work of Welcoming Families include the whole movement?

In the sense that, not only in Milan or Chiavari, but also in Rome or in Catanzaro, the families that are interested in hospitality depend on this group. Grow as much as you like: the preoccupations that have been expressed here are valid for the movement anywhere. What is more, a work that interests the whole nation (and the movement is spread out everywhere) has a social and even political impact that is much greater. Therefore, I always say to the Union of the Families[31] that either it is strictly functional, for example for Welcoming Families and the problems that pertain to them, or else it will be limited and dry up: there should be a connection. Welcoming Families is the only work that is for families. The Union of Families cannot be conceived of and act, in my opinion, in a parallel fashion, or purely collaterally. It should be "in function of." Now, in function of what? The functionality should be a greater action, a greater possibility for helping, a greater diffusion of Welcoming Families. Conversely, Welcoming Families will be the first ones to be interested in the battle if, for example, the Union of Families is working for family benefits or for freedom in education. The problem of school, of education, is also grafted onto this.

The ideal of man is not the family; the ideal of man is that he be whole. Therefore, we are interested in the problem of education, the problem of a fair wage. And this is a very important corollary—which pertains to the Popular Movement[32]—that has its roots in a charity toward man that characterizes Christian education.

I am really grateful to you: few things are as useful as this work. And then what a surprise that there are a thousand families, whereas before I thought there were only a few. So, the service of the central leadership becomes very important: it is an enormous service that reverberates from your personal initiative.

A second "nota bene." I ask you to use *Litterae Communionis*: people need to know about it![33] Help people learn about it! Because someone can be encouraged to bear her illness, the cancer that is in its last stage, hearing these things; someone can be supported in the labor of his faith.

What kind of work should be included in Welcoming Families? For example, a family arrives from Peru and, unfortunately, I cannot take them into my house. . . .

My answer is that first of all the identification of areas where Welcoming Families can work should be taken care of by the relevant community. This is the first "canvassing" to do.

If in every city or in every large area there were two, three, twenty-seven families available, afterward you can do a census: in this census, the families that have exceptional circumstances, that is, the minority, or the parents, or the family members of the sick people that are in the hospital, should come together in unity within your Association. The others shouldn't; the others can take part in a bigger list, so that if my friend has to go to Tirano, he can turn to a family there.

We need to do a first count: the identification of leaders in individual cities, of families that are geared toward younger children, toward some need, an objective need, a physical need. These should enter into your Association, and the others, the families that welcome in a general sense, should be part of a bigger list. Only, I would distinguish the Association proper from this list, so as not to create an elephantine and useless organism that is not necessary, at least not for now.

And when we find ourselves in front of people who ask us for companionship, to accompany them in difficult situations?

This is something that the community or the Fraternity can take care of. There can be emergencies or doubts or questions that can be handled at this level. For example: there is a girl who is going to give birth, who is a young mother, and has a vocational problem, the problem of her future: she cannot come here, to Welcoming Families, automatically. Developing a relationship with her, you can invite her to your Fraternity. I say that the problem is a problem for the Fraternity or the community, except in cases of a personal relationship that you take on.

Yesterday, at the meeting for the end of the year, the third point was "freedom from the outcome." How does this touch on what we are living?

Freedom from the outcome makes it possible for charity to be the real motivation. But this is true for any relationship that man lives in relation with the Infinite, with God. In relationship with God, there is no measure, and therefore, there is no outcome. Thus, the publican went home from the Temple blessed by God, and he was a "dirty sinner," as they all said. Without this freedom from the outcome, one can't even begin. One is handicapped from the start.

The temptation for us, at least for me, is to see this initiative as something independent. I understood instead that there is no truth and newness with respect to hospitality unless it refers to a truth and a newness that I live by following the movement. I think this is a fundamental question because the risk is often that of becoming autonomous with respect to the origin that is much bigger than this thing to which we dedicate ourselves. The risk is that we create a specialist association.

Whether the Association becomes specialist or not does not depend so much on the way you design the work but on who you are. If you are immersed in the experience of faith, the experience of the movement, then what you do will also feel like it is a part and an expression of the life of the community. And in fact, the logic is very clear: "We welcome because we have been welcomed." Anyone can say it: "Lord make me understand how I am made because I am not only nature or history. I am welcomed!" We welcome because we have been welcomed. As Saint John said: "We love because we have been loved." This and only this is what should be happening here, otherwise we can be as generous as we want, we can give ourselves over to the flames—as Saint Paul said—and be worth nothing. To give away all your money, your own body to the flames, if you don't have love, is not worth anything. What is charity? It is the recognition that we are loved. It is the recognition of Christ, that is, that God has loved us. Someone, speaking in a Christian way, should welcome the difficulty of his work because he is welcomed, feels himself welcomed by Christ. Therefore, charity is born of the flesh.

How do we make sacrifices in freedom and joy?

If you cannot make a sacrifice, if you do it without joy, it is better not to do it! But I can only answer you by using the word "recognition." After twenty years of marriage, even after fifteen, ten, or less, what there is between a man and a woman is a profound recognition which cannot be compared to the original affection because it is even greater, even if it is different. As the poet Ada Negri, who

I always quote, says in *My Youth*: "I haven't lost you. You've stayed deep in my being. It is you, but you're another"—even greater![34]

This observation is very precious. It is a preoccupation that I always have, and I have it from the strictly moral point of view: we should not measure. To each his own, his dimension, in his availability to God. And you do not know what will be asked of you tomorrow. As a phrase from Giancarlo Puecher says (he died as a partisan insurgent and was truly a great Christian): "Protect me, God, because starting this morning I do not know where I will be this evening." This availability is true greatness.

Thank you very much. I encourage you not to let a day go by without praying to the Virgin Mary. When people come and ask me: "What should we do?" I respond: "Say a prayer or even only a Hail Mary every day together." And they say to me: "Is that it?" In any case, let us say a Hail Mary for our families.

Embracing What Is Different

WHEN ONE GETS OLD, one becomes wiser, and thinking about God becomes habitual; one understands that it would be useless to do anything, if not for God. Let us say therefore a prayer to the Virgin, the first who welcomed in herself the "great difference" when she welcomed God in herself.

I wanted to come above all to hear your interventions—whether these are made in the form of a descriptive testimony or of a more or less anxious question—and to let myself react to you because I understand in your words how all your gestures of welcoming are full of your imitation of God.

Yours is not first of all an organization, but an *experience*; the word "experience" indicates the connection that our action has with its ultimate source, the mystery of God. It is in experience that God enriches our nothingness and forgives our misery, making it act, making it participate in His "activity" (a banal word, but we haven't been able to find a better one) as Creator, Re-creator, Redeemer. Experience always affirms a connection with God. In fact, an experience becomes evil when this nexus with God is not recognized and our work is tempted to prescind from God or go against the law of God: an experience that does not respect the great source from which every human energy is born cannot last long.

"The one who does, fails"[35]—but within that same failure comes the goodness of a Redemption through the humility of accepting forgiveness, through the contrition that comes when we recognize our errors. It is through failure that normally—I say normally—man walks toward God. It is the system that God has used. At the beginning of the human story, He allowed (we say this humanly speaking) a mysterious, tremendous thing—something that presses on every person who comes into the world, the anguish, in the Latin sense of the word, that presses on his throat, chokes him, on a path that otherwise would have been wide and peaceful: I mean original sin. Because of original sin, God became one of us, this history that God wanted to build brought Him to live within our flesh.

Yours is an experience, therefore it is a connection with the divine. It is connection with the Mystery. But let's not use abstract words anymore, let's use words that come from our history: it is a connection between you and Christ, between you and God made man.

The Experience of Companionship

Only from an experience can the desire to help each other be born, and it is normal for it to be born in this way. Your experience is a *companionship*, even before it is an organization or a structure. Experience implicates and puts in play your I, your person, not your adhesion to an association. Your person, with the fire of love and sacrifice that inspires it, can remain more open, with a sensitivity to sacrifice and to the joy of others. Thus, the life of friendship consists of this ease in supporting each other.

Yours is an experience and it is a friendship. The organization and the Association is an instrument to help these two things: personal experience and mutual friendship.

Experience and friendship (or companionship) that are born from experience have a characteristic that demonstrates their closeness to Christ. Experience is a horizon that is always growing: the more one penetrates experience by welcoming it, the more one walks in it, the more this enlarges itself, with a horizon that becomes ever greater. The companionship is a friendship that we live in this fleeting world, but with a value that is not fleeting, the relationship with Christ.

"Therefore"—Saint Paul says in the Letter to the Hebrews— "since we are surrounded by so great a cloud of witnesses" (Hebrews 12:1): The Church is truly a great people made up of witnesses! So many times, the temptation comes to separate the little things from the great things, but the little things are so dense, so intense, that there is no longer little and great—everything is great. I have seen a young mother who tried to feed her fussy child by doing tricks with a spoon: this is something divine, great like God! Therefore, I am a little embarrassed in coming to talk to you.

"Therefore, since we are surrounded by so great a cloud of witnesses, let us also lay aside every weight": we can throw off what hinders us by living; if someone does not want to live, then he does not throw it off and the hindrance defines him.

"Let us also lay aside every weight, and sin which clings so closely": we are not the ones who redeem ourselves; our struggle to come to the aid of those in need, of the life that is always in front of us, between our arms, is not a gesture that can redeem our life, that can redeem the world. Even if we are barely attentive to what is really going on, we no longer feel the temptation to pride, to a moralistic satisfaction with ourselves. We are able to perceive very well the strange commingling of the desire to be generous—which pursues the good and the true that we recognize—along with the tiredness and the errors that penetrate our work.

"Therefore, since we are surrounded by so great a cloud of witnesses, let us also lay aside every weight, and sin which clings so closely, and let us run with perseverance the race that is set before us." "Let us run with perseverance": the word perseverance recalls the great word that Christ repeated, more than all the others, in his last discourse, a word which made his disciples capable of giving up their lives: remain, stay, remain in me.

"Let us run with perseverance the race that is set before us": if one goes to the very end, it is not because one has built something definitive; after so much time, one understands that he is still only at the beginning. The one who goes to the end is an instrument of the arm of God in the world and therefore collaborates in the final redemption when everything that went astray will return to how it was in the mind of God the Creator, and everything that was filthy and heavy will become light and free, and everything that seemed on the point of dying, or that suffocated our life from one moment to the next, will become life, life eternal.

Being Available

In another passage from the Letter to the Hebrews, Saint Paul describes this path on which we should run with perseverance: "Let brotherly love continue" (Hebrews 13:1).

You speak of your babies, of your children, those of your flesh and those not of your own flesh, because in the end, it is the same thing: the Second Vatican Council reminds us that the first characteristic of a Christian family is its availability for adoption. In adoption, we typically see what Saint John said on the first page of his Gospel, when he speaks of those "born, not of blood nor of the will of the flesh nor of the will of man, but of God." (Cf. John 1:13.). So the children of flesh come from God, just like the children whose needs have raised up in you this mysterious and miraculous pity, and you embraced them and brought them with you.

"Let brotherly love continue. Do not neglect to show hospitality to strangers" (Hebrews 13:1-2). The word *hospitality* or *welcome* has to do with the whole *person*. This is the difference of hospitality when compared to all other forms of charity; it is a charity to the person, it has to do directly with the person as such.

If someone has a broken foot and you help him, you help that person who has a broken foot. When you adopt or take in a child, more considerably and visibly, it is precisely the person who is the object of the gesture.

"Do not neglect to show hospitality to strangers, for thereby some have entertained angels unawares" (Hebrews 13:2). Saint Paul is referring to several passages from the Old Testament. But after Christ we can say: "Remember that, by practicing hospitality, you have welcomed, even without being aware of it, the angel of God, you have welcomed the presence of God, the way in which God has become a presence in your life."

We cannot let our welcoming of other people become something abstract, because welcoming has as its proper object, before any broken limb or fractured psyche, the person who is welcomed. Even without knowing it and even without thinking about it, God has sent this person to you. And, welcoming her, you welcome Christ.

I hope that you are used to re-reading the twenty-fifth chapter of Saint Matthew's Gospel to console yourselves in your labor and to comfort yourselves in your human errors. Hospitality is a sign, the norm of any other kind of charity: *to welcome another means to welcome Christ.*

Welcoming Something Different

But I wanted to linger on a point that in this dialogue may serve as a point of comparison and a confirmation or may reveal the nature of your work: *hospitality always means welcoming something different from us.* The deepest dimension for which welcoming others makes us similar to God who creates and redeems is in the reality of *difference,* the fact that the other does not coincide with what we imagined, what we may like, what might console us.

It is welcoming one who is different from us that makes us similar to God. Is there a greater difference than that between being and nothingness? This is an infinite difference. The Infinite created us from nothing, welcomed you and me out of nothing; we were nothing and God welcomed you and me. "Our Father, you are in my depths, from whom I am born and am"[36] (the tenth chapter of *The Religious Sense* says this, which I hope we have meditated on; if we have not done so, then I ask you to go and look at it again).

Is there something more dramatically and terribly different than the difference between being and nothingness? More terrible still is the difference between God made man for love of the men He had welcomed—God welcomed us by becoming man and embraced us, in the literal sense of the term, in so far as baptism is precisely a permanent and eternal physical embrace—the man who is a sinner. More terrible is this difference between absolute purity, between absolute truth and beauty and the sinner.

As I get older, one of the two or three things that keep me going deeper in a fascinating way, that fill me with fear and trembling, is not so much the concept, but the experience of being a sinner. Is there a greater difference than that between the Father who created me and my forgetfulness and my denial, my sin?

Welcoming as the embrace of what is different: I use this experience to define the word *forgiveness*. Welcoming is really forgiving, the embrace of difference. To welcome is to forgive: it is the same. In this sense, in your house, the first welcome, and therefore the first forgiveness, is with your wife and with your husband.

Welcoming is *the embrace of what is different*, and for this reason it has to do with all our relationships. The embrace of difference is called "forgiveness," because to embrace someone different demands first that we forgive him. To forgive means to affirm, under all the ugliness, what is true and right, good and beautiful, to affirm the being that is in the other: the being of the other. Your being is greater and deeper, more important than thousands, than thousands upon thousands, of your sins. It is the concept that John Paul II expressed in his encyclical *Dives in Misericordia*.[37]

The Imitation of Christ

How much work we have to do to accept these things every day—which are the greatest things that we can talk about as human beings—in a way that is so inadequate! Pure gratuitousness in this embrace is impossible. For this reason, Saint Paul speaks about sin that besieges us. Pure gratuitousness in welcoming, in forgiving, in the relationship with your wife or in the relationship with an adopted child, in whatever condition he or she may be, even in the worst situations (substantially the structure of the question is the same), is not possible: gratuitousness is not possible if we are not moved by the love of Christ.

In the twenty-fifth chapter of Saint Matthew, we find these incredibly consoling words: "Come, O blessed of my Father, inherit the kingdom prepared for you from the foundation of the world; for I was hungry and you gave me food. . ." (Matthew 25:34ff). How is this possible? We have never seen you! "As you did it to one of the least of these my brethren, you did it to me." Even without thinking of Him directly, it could be just the purity with which I encounter the other, a husband or a wife or any person in need that you welcome and embrace in hospitality (don't be scandalized if I use the comparison of the husband-wife relationship, because deep down it is true); welcoming a different type of person could be a gratuitousness ; it could be a truly gratuitous and pure desire to help, even without thinking of Christ: but still it is a miracle that Christ is doing. Christ can do miracles even without our becoming aware of it; but others become aware of it, as I was reminded when I saw that young mother feeding the fussy child. This is why I said: "God, make me like this mother."

Anyway, we cannot be gratuitous without Christ, without love for Christ. When the desire to help is a grace, it is a miracle that Christ is working in a person; it means that this person sooner or later will come face to face with Christ and say: "You were within that guy, that friend, you were within the person that I welcomed, and I didn't know it. I thank you, Christ, for helping me accomplish something I would never have accomplished alone."

We cannot live in welcome except for love of Christ. The love of Christ means *imitating Christ.* The supreme comparison, the supreme example of welcome, is God who had such pity on man that He became one of us and died for us: Redemption. Any gesture of hospitality is an echo of this.

To welcome the other, to love the other, is to imitate Christ, to welcome Christ. Doing what you do is loving God, loving Christ, affirming the fact that existence is positive, that God exists, affirming that in existence goodness wins, Christ wins. The more you live this generosity with awareness, the more your generosity will not be at the mercy of your desires, of your tiredness, of your feelings. Otherwise, feeling, instinct, how things seem to be going, will be the measure of what you do. And, when you reach your limit, you say: "No, it's not possible to do anything else; I cannot do this." Therefore, I made the comparison with the relationship between a man and a woman: only with Christ can the relationship between a man and a woman be indissoluble. It is made to be indissoluble, but only with Christ can it be like this. Only with Christ can the act of generosity with which you practice hospitality go to the very end.

Fighting for Humanity

A "nota bene." The awareness of the relationship with Christ multiplies the strength of imagination, multiplies the energy of dedication, makes us persevere. Chapters eight and nine of the Second Letter of Saint Paul to the Corinthians say this, show us the way to be charitable.

The love of Christ can even lead you to say with peace and humility, "I cannot go beyond this, I cannot do it," and make you reach a sense of your limits, make you so free, and so humble, that you understand how poor man is, that you understand your own poverty, so that when you see the Albanians after crossing the Adriatic Sea, being rejected and sent back, you are not able to do anything. It is something that can leave me in peace only if I offer Christ the pain of my limits and of those people and say: "Lord, this has to do with the mysterious design with which you began creation, permitting evil, injustice, disaster, and you will direct it to good." But I must not, as so often happens, forget these things, make myself forget the flood in Bangladesh or the drama in Lebanon or in Albania.

Only the love of Christ allows us to have the supreme, gratu-itous purity that is humility, the humility of my own limits. My limits will not mean ungenerosity, will not weigh on my con-science like a sin: to recognize my own limits will be another type of hospitality. Through the welcome of what we are unable to do,

I welcome the mystery of God who makes everything. It is God who saves, who makes us safe, makes us live, leads us to eternal life. Therefore, even a word of comfort— "Courage!"—has an eternal value.

What I am saying does not seem abstract to me, because sooner or later, to live reasonably, as a man, one has to remember these things. All these observations make us great, in the eyes of this fraternal outsider, make us ready to help your work with the little we can understand, even with a word like "courage." What an amazing thing it is to watch!

When I receive certain letters, for minutes at a time I am not able to do anything else; and when there is some gathering, I read the most recent ones I've received. And you have to excuse me if I only answer a few, because my old age weighs on me and makes it more difficult to do what I have to do.

"We have become a spectacle to the world, to angels and to men" (1 Corinthians 4:9). There is nothing more human on this earth than the Church of God, and in this there is nothing more human than the hospitality that you are living. It is a sign, not only for the ones you welcome, because you are a sign for all of us. The whole life of the Church, the whole life of the Christian people, should be a welcoming in the way that you have understood it, in pulling down the walls of resistance and sustaining lives that otherwise the world would erase.

The most beautiful thing in our movement is the reality of your friendship that gives life to this hospitality, precisely because it is a sign, like a flag that calls everyone into battle. What are we fighting for? For humanity, for eternity.

The other day I saw a "foreigner" who came up to these two kids who were speaking among themselves in order to ask them for something. The kids told him that they didn't have anything, and he went away. I asked the person who was with me to run after him; he found him and gave him a few bucks. How many needs in this world should we run after like that!

The Imitation of Christ

WE WANTED TO MEET WITH YOU and get your help to do better what we are doing, that is, to be ever more aware and responsible for the work of our Association. We are asking for your help on three points. First of all, we want to ask you why you so often use the experience of Welcoming Families as an example for the whole movement, whose "objective" impact is not so relevant: we are only 2,000 families!

One of you would be enough!

What is the "kernel" of our experience of welcome, the value to which you draw the attention of the whole movement?

First of all, thank you for your invitation. Maybe I shouldn't have accepted it, because you need people who are involved in an experience like yours: only the one who is more mature in the experience that we have, in fact, can help us.

This first question, though, gives me breath: to ask ourselves the motivation for an act of charity means to put out in the open the very reason for saying that charity is the law of life. Therefore, even if these are things that I already said on other occasions, *repetita iuvant* [repetition does us good]: if you've repeated the question, you will permit me to repeat the answer.

To welcome another person, in the full sense of the word, means to open your life to the boundaries of the life of this person, including her in the same boundaries of your life. It does not have to do with giving someone something to eat, of spending an hour together, of giving someone a place to sleep: it has to do with giving food, a bed, welcoming for an hour, being attentive when someone cries, being attentive when she laughs, being attentive to her need, exactly as—the comparison is unique—we do for a child. The welcoming of which Welcoming Families speaks is the welcome of a mother and a father for their children, of a brother for a brother, like the poem "I due orfani" by Pascoli, where the mother and father have died and only the two brothers remain. First of all, then, welcoming implies and indicates a totality of embrace, a totality of interest. It is truly in welcoming another that the formula "Love another as yourself" is applied, even physically, formally, precisely as a form.

I intend to speak to Welcoming Families only in so far as this totalization of welcoming can be planned for. I can welcome, everybody can welcome, but the kind of welcome that you give either demands a whole family or creates a family in an analogous sense. The family is the first phenomenon, by nature, in which welcoming another takes on these all-encompassing characteristics. It could be that a single person could welcome a child or welcome a young person as if he were a child: analogically, a family would form.

So I permit myself to insist on the value of hospitality, because the totalizing nature expresses the essence of the greatest virtue, to which all the other values in life make reference—the virtue of charity, that is, of gratuitous love, of the love that is not generated or sustained by a calculation or an advantage, even if there can be advantages, but it is not lived for the advantages, or for a calculation. Hospitality assumes the virtue of charity, thus realizing to the ultimate degree the very nature of the human dynamic, the human dynamism of imitating God, that is of realizing the ideal of love. In this phenomenon, the whole mystery of the Trinity reverberates, because the mystery of the Trinity is—analogically speaking—an infinite hospitality, an all-encompassing infinity, and an infinite gratuitousness. This last observation reflects nothing other than the value of man's life in so far as he imitates God, which means the virtue of love—of love in so far as it is totalizing and totally gratuitous in its genesis, in its motivation, totally gratuitous as imitation of God, of the mystery of God.

It is for this reason that I make such a big deal out of Welcoming Families: it doesn't matter if there are two thousand or three. If there were only one, I would use it as an example. There is no other comparison because in every other instance of sharing life, there is a partiality that here in your families, by definition, there cannot be.

Isn't it a partial sharing when we give temporary hospitality? For example, a foster child or the case of a baby who is with us for only a month. . . .

The point is the nature of the relationship. The length of the fostering, or of the hospitality, if it does not depend on you, that is, if it is not an influence on the decision, does not determine the decision, does not take away the fact that the availability you are giving is total: it would be a total availability even if you gave it for only thirty days, instead of three hundred thousand. Therefore, I don't think that the limit of time takes away the value of the thing.

If the limit doesn't become a part of your decision. . . .

I said: "If the limit is not an influence on the decision" because the value of a virtue is in the totality of availability, in the total openness that man offers to God, with which man offers himself to a situation and therefore to God. The true application, the true realization of the value of hospitality, is there where, because it does not depend on us, there is no limit; it does not have a limit in the way we live together every day, as it doesn't have limits in time and space. This is how it is for children.

Therefore, this question is important, because your effort, in the sense of *ascesis*—"effort" is the word that translates the Greek word *ascesis* and which means, in terms of your life, *virtue*—your effort, your *ascesis*, your dedication, should aim not for silencing your guilt (the guilt you may feel in front of the need of another and his lack of help), should not tend toward an egocentric or prideful satisfaction, should not make us say, like the Pharisee: I do all these things, I am good, others don't do them (cf. Luke 18:11.). In your gesture, the availability should be at play so that you can imitate the love of God.

Without the awareness of the imitation of the love of God, of the love that God has for us, we cannot even love our children well: there would be a limit beyond which we would not be able to tolerate, we would love our children in the measure that they correspond to an image that we made of them.

With this observation, I want to say that the value of hospitality is in the totalizing generosity, in the all-encompassing openness of the heart that offers itself. If it were not like this, the individual we welcome would easily suffer injustice, would suffer from our limits, would be destined to suffer the defects of our character (he will suffer them all the same, but it is different: even we suffer the defects of our character, but we don't plan them in advance!).

In short, welcoming another is the ethical phenomenon that most imitates what Christ is for man, what Christ is for every man. Jesus did not ask Zacchaeus—the story of Zacchaeus is my favorite passage of the Gospel—"Listen up, give back what you have taken, be good, don't rob anymore," but rather simply told him: "I must stay at your house today" (Luke 19:5), that is, "I am with you." Hospitality is this "being with." Therefore, moralism is the opposite of Christianity. Christianity was not born as the preaching of virtue but as the welcoming of a presence. If you welcome this presence, you are obliged to follow certain virtues, otherwise, you are not really welcoming it.

You said: "Hospitality is the ethical phenomenon that most imitates. . . ." I find in myself the risk almost of a presumption, of a pretense in front of others, having the attitude of scolding them because they do not adhere to this phenomenon that "more than all the others" imitates Christ.

This is how the Pharisee judged. I was saying that hospitality has all its value if the limits in which it lives, in which it is constrained to live, are not put up with or planned in advance by us; there can be a welcome that lasts a minute and which is totalizing. It is all-encompassing when someone welcomes the other according to the totality of her being, of her existence, therefore lives the charity that God has with her, the charity of God toward her, the love of God for her, the acceptance and sustenance of her in everything that she lives, in all the moments of her life. In short, what characterizes hospitality as a value is this totality. This totality is not an object, but rather a fullness, the wideness of an embrace from the heart, which can only touch the totality of the presence of the other.

Can you elaborate on this aspect of the limit set by us?

If you are given a child to foster, let's say, for one month. You, in that month, truly live hospitality, because your heart has an openness that is not fixed or measured by a month. Therefore, I say that if you hold a baby for one minute, you can hold him in true hospitality if you give him the totality of your "I," if you do not block your embrace according to your own preoccupations. Anyway, the response to this question, formally, is that hospitality is the greatest imitation that man can live of the love that God brings to men, therefore of the same love that constitutes the life of God: a totality of availability in front of a totality of presence.

The value of hospitality is supported by an incredibly simple attitude. I think that there is nothing closer to the first beatitude: "Blessed are the poor in spirit, for theirs is the kingdom of heaven" (Matthew 5:3). Hospitality is a type of poverty; it doesn't have anything to save beforehand and therefore does not make any calculation.

The second question is connected to what we have already said. How is it possible for us to be more transparent, to be like leaven for the movement, for the community, for our society, transparent to this value (that, as you have said, the value is for everyone, it is not only a vocation that touches a few families and that's it)?

Exactly. You are leaven for everyone in the measure you live this welcome with all the availability of your heart; you are leaven in the community as an example that the others see and carry out as they can, according to the measure of their freedom (which God judges) and according to the measure of God's grace. Therefore, there is nothing more opposed to the merits of hospitality than making the comparisons about which we spoke earlier, or of demanding that other people have this same experience. Not demanding it is a great maturity, requires a great sacrifice, the sacrifice of not being attached to the good in which we are engaged, of not being attached to our own virtue, demands that we be without pride. Even if the whole world were living hospitality, a hospitality like Jesus Christ taught us, the world would be a place of unhappy people all the same. Because ultimate happiness is beyond this. As the gardener said in Miguel Mañara: "Everything is where it should be and goes where it should go: to the place assigned by a wisdom that (Heaven be praised!) is not ours."[38] It is so beautiful to respond to God through what He asks of us, respecting, loving, and esteeming all around us!

Living hospitality however can also be something done in silence and obscurity. We have become aware, in these ten years of our history, how important it is to speak, to give witness to what the Lord has given us to live.

It is important to give witness in so far as that witness can become a word that is comprehensible and shocking for others. If you say a word that does not draw the attention of anyone, what you say is useless. There is an exceptionality of situation that gives witness to the virtue even in something normal, that is a virtue even if it is ordinary, that has merit even if it is lived every day over a long period of time. Then there can be an occasion when this everyday virtue suddenly breaks out in an exceptional way: this is the occasion when we should give testimony. To be always in front, always pushing people out of the way to say what we are doing, just to be happy that we've said it, this is not a merit, and it doesn't strike anyone.

You are an example for the community, in the first place, when you live: living we are an example, and "let the one who has ears hear it and the one who has eyes see it" (cf. Mark 4:9ff.); we are an example given over to the good will of others. In the second place, we give an example to the community by proclaiming an event or a fact that is so exceptional in its happening that it cannot but arouse surprise in people, call them back from distraction, strike the awareness of people. It is the concept of miracle. Jesus introduced His presence among us through miracles. But the miracle implies an exceptionality, and the corresponding reaction, the corresponding shock. The more one was sensitive and attentive, silent and attentive, conscious and attentive, the more everything that Jesus did became a miracle. For the crowd, something great had happened, feeding them by multiplying bread so they didn't have to go buy any. In fact, Jesus told them: "You came looking for me because you got free bread. But I came not to give you free bread"—the point is not to fix the Italian or the European economy—"I came to give you another bread, myself" (cf. John 6:26ff).

We had a third question. We wanted your judgment on a proposal, a hypothesis which we discussed together the last time in Florence. It is a proposal that is somewhat preparatory to hospitality, that enlarges the setting of love for this virtue, of availability to the richness of this experience. Many families have difficulties that are also logistical, or anyway they do not have for now the openness to a total hospitality like that which you spoke about (it is not our business to judge). So, we thought about offering some more limited gestures that do not possess the totality to which you called us, but which can be a way for someone to share the experience we live in first person: for example, helping someone do the ironing rather than taking the child to catechism class, or helping with math homework, babysitting, etc.: to offer this possibility to more families that in some way leads them to live more closely the experience of hospitality. We wanted you to help us judge this proposal and to understand its limits better because there are also the charitable works of various communities and we do not want to take their place. [39]

There is also the fact that many people who meet us want to get involved in our gestures.

Let's say that in your Association there are 103 host families in thirty-four cities. In these thirty-four cities, there are people who, seeing the work you do, say: "I also want to collaborate in your work; therefore I will iron the clothes or do the shopping every day." This is a real participation, if it is conscious, of the virtue of hospitality, because the motive for which these people offer themselves is that of helping you in the work that you have begun, that you have accepted to do. The motive for which someone offers himself is that of helping you in the task you have taken up: it is eminently singular the help they offer to you and your family in that determined condition. The openness to charitable work, instead, is different: to help others—which normally is organized in reference to a center of the community, the center of the charitable work—of whom it is said: "Look, there are these two host families that need you to help with the washing," and they agree to give this service. The origin of this acceptance is not a reaction full of esteem for the virtue of hospitality but is more directly an openness to charity, so much so that if a week later, the head of the charitable work says: "Look, there is a more serious case that needs help," the person, making herself available, leaves this first work to go to the other one.

The first group of people participate in the reality of hospitality as a virtue, as an attitude that is chosen and desired. For this reason, I underlined the singularity of the help offered. They see your wife close to burnout and say: "We will take on ourselves a part of the work of your hospitality." These participate in the totality of your hospitality. They also make up part of Welcoming Families. But the others do not; the others are part of the movement, of a cooperative of charity.

The Association as such has as its ultimate aim the promotion of an ideal. Whoever says to you "we will help carry a part of your weight" participates in the ideal. In order to do a charitable work, it is not necessary to be a member of the Welcoming Families Association. In fact, there can be one within the Association who welcomes more people than she can, more children than he can, and be full of recrimination toward others, as the president told us just now: she can be full of demands toward others because they don't do this work.

Many families, through the testimonies we give, are fascinated by the position that is behind this work and show admiration and interest in our experience. Often, after months of participating or after a few years, they also open themselves up for some gesture.

Even these are part of Welcoming Families because they have not closed themselves off—deep down there is an openness, however uncertain and childish, but still an openness. When it matures, they work.

However, the principal thing to underline is that the value of hospitality, the adequate reason for welcoming a person, is that this person is created and loved by God, is saved and redeemed by Christ, is part of the mystery of Christ, is part of the body of Christ. For this reason, we exclude any claim or demand toward the person we welcome (even if there are demands all the same; there are also such things between husband and wife!).

As *The Religious Sense* says, the heart of man is relationship with the Infinite: there is no other value than the relationship lived with the Infinite.[40] Therefore, there would be no value in giving our body to the flames, giving all that we have to the poor, it would not be worth it to sacrifice everything, says Saint Paul in the thirteenth chapter of the First Letter to the Corinthians, if not for charity (cf. 1 Corinthians 13). What is this "charity" which is greater than any possible or imaginable sacrifice (like that of Jan Palach in Prague, for example, who let himself be burned for an ideal)? This charity is the love of Being, the love of God. Why is it love of God? Because God is the totalizing reason, total gratuitousness: charity is the answer to the gratuitousness that created us. As is always the case, living an act of virtue like welcoming a stranger pushes you to rethink even the way you live with your wife, purifies the reason you live with your husband; but it also purifies the reason you live in the community, and corrects the image the newspapers give of us.

Therefore, let us never let a day go by without asking the Virgin Mary for the grace to know how to welcome what is given to us because we cannot do anything on our own (just look at those who get married: after a little bit, they just put up with each other, which is the ugliest thing there is)!

We have many friends who are in difficulty and who want to be with us because they feel helped in carrying their daily burdens.

This is not a participation in the Association. They can very well participate in all the meetings they want. Let them! As long as there are not 500 who participate in this way and only two who do the work of welcoming.

If hospitality is the ethical and moral event that most makes us imitate the Lord, there will probably be help that flows out to others as well. Therefore, we should not suffocate the Spirit. But participating in the Association as such is not this. Pray to the Virgin Mary that even I may participate with you, even without being part of the Association.

In the companionship we offer each other—which is so important for all of us, to carry the weight, but more still to call us to what you clearly indicated today as the why and thus the how; from the why comes the how—all of us can testify personally how even our concrete life has changed. When new people come, though, who may be far from the movement, who do not necessarily start out from the perspective of faith, but only from a need (for example, the fact that they are trying to adopt or have a young girl to look after), our companionship would need to be capable of helping these people in terms of a closeness that would become a kind of paternity: a taking charge of the other "host family," with all that this means, walking alongside their freedom, which is un-touchable, to help them understand what it means to say yes or to say no to the proposal that is made to them by the social service or by the need that they encounter. So, I wanted to hear you on this topic of assuming responsibility for those who are not part of our history.

If there is an Association and it has a meaning, it is because its members help each other to live the aim of that Association: to help the freedom of the other fulfill what led him to this openness. To help the openness of the other means also to tell him why we do this work. The other can adopt a child from natural instinct, for the sake of a natural need. And then he hears you say that the motive for accepting this adoptive child, exactly as if she had been born to you, the only motive that explains this is the love of God, obedience to God! This must be said. To help means also to explain the why behind the things you do. It also means helping the children grow up, by telling them the reason why you put them in that environment. To help anyone who is in your Association is the right thing to do because of the very aim of the Association. In the second place, in particular, I permit myself to observe that the greatest help is to illuminate the other on the true "why," the reason why his generosity is set in motion. Thus, in fact, the Lord makes Himself known: first, He gives us life; by living, we encounter a question, we live the impact with reality that sustains our question, whose answer is the existence of the Lord.

Today, we heard the word paternity. This strikes me as odd, as I am a woman.

Everything that is destined to transform, moving another toward its fulfillment, is paternity or maternity, which is the same thing: it means to generate. To move another to be ever more complete is to generate. The ultimate ideal of a friendly relationship between two people is paternity or maternity, and this is the ideal that our contemporary culture tries to block and suffocate. Thus, there is no friendship between people. The ideal of friendship is called paternity or maternity. The father is the one who brings life for the sake of happiness, the mother is the one who brings life for the sake of happiness: fruitfulness is to put that fullness which is happiness on the right path, and friendship is the companionship guided toward happiness, as we always say.

It is a paternity that is reflected by the fuller paternity in the movement and in the Church.

This applies within a particular vocation, which is eminently personal, what the mystery of the Church of God is for the whole world and what a piece of the Church like our movement lives.

If paternity and maternity are not joined by the feeling of companionship and the affection of a relationship, they are still not true. Thus, the *Memores Domini*, who consecrate themselves to God, if they do not live paternity or maternity, are not true even within their vocation. To direct another more and more toward his or her destiny is paternity or maternity. A mother or a father who physically generate a child and then abandon that child after three days evidently are neither father nor mother. It is for this reason that a man and a woman who do not have children and who adopt a son are truly the father and the mother in the measure that they educate that child. Much more than that great majority who pop out of the womb a child and do not educate him, do not take care for his destiny.

Familiarity as the Method
of the Mystery

I THANK YOU AGAIN FOR HAVING given us this chance to meet with you. The national leaders of the Welcoming Families Association are gathered here: they are the point of paternity, of responsibility, of judgment, and of companionship that is most true to the life of our Association. They have each brought their questions; I will synthesize them for you because there are so many.

In order to take up again the thread of a conversation that you had with us more than three years ago, in November 1992 [the preceding chapter, "Imitating Christ"], *I wanted to call to mind the things you said on that occasion.*

You were saying that welcoming people into our families, which is what characterizes the experience of the families in our Association, implies a totality of embrace. You insisted on this totality because it represents the ethical phenomenon that most closely imitates the initiative of Christ for man. So, this experience of welcoming people into our families requires in us the availability of heart to imitate the love of God, and in this sense it is a virtue (a virtue not only for us but also for others; but we are called to live it in a very precise way). You added that in the measure we live this hospitality with all the availability of our heart, we are a leaven for the community, for the world, without making any demands on the others—we can be a leaven by living and testifying, where testimony means to tell about an experience that is so distinctive that it cannot but move others. In this sense, maybe, we can use the term "miracle" as you recalled the last time.

You then said that the Association serves to help us flesh out for each other the ultimate why of our experience—which is obedience to God—and that in helping each other to have this awareness, we live a reciprocal relationship of responsibility (among ourselves and with our other associates) which must become a paternity.

In these two years, we have worked a lot—even as a Governing Board—on what you have been teaching little by little to the leadership assemblies.[41] *In particular, the calls you made for unity in leading and for community—not in the sense of a democracy, but as a way of conceiving of ourselves differently—have been really important for us. And it seems to me that for most of us, there has been a rediscovery here of a dimension of fraternity that is greater than any worrying about gestures or the organization of the Association as a work. Even if, in this fraternal dimension among us, it has also truly augmented the care we have for particulars that we are given to live, a capacity for creativity and effectiveness.*

I ask you: How can the Association, in the specific details, experience more the particular awareness that the movement is living at this time?

This question seems so fundamental to me that I want to linger here for a moment. Then we can go on with all the particulars you want.

First of all, I am the one who should thank you for what I am about to say. In these times, I have been surprised by the fact that I understand, at seventy-three years of age, things that I have always said: at seventy-three years of age, I realize that I only understand them now. There is an increase in comprehension, which is a sign of life. In this sense, the phrase is true (when I brought it to mind yesterday, it reanimated me), which spoke about the person who died young: "Death is young." Not just to say this beautiful phrase again: because it is a beautiful phrase if it is true; otherwise, it is a really ugly phrase.

I wanted to communicate something to you about the things that I have discovered in these months and that I hadn't understood before as I understand them now. I asked myself the other day: How did John and Andrew, in that late afternoon, looking at

Jesus, begin something that would fill the world and all time, so much so that it has arrived at this point? I am still speaking about it; we are all thinking about it. Reading that page of the Gospel of John, we read something that is much more pertinent, present, comforting, pressing, and sparking of hope than any other page written in this world. How did those two fishermen, those two peasants (who became five or six in a couple of days), get to where they got? Saint James got as far as a place called "Santiago de Compostela," which was the extreme limit of the known Western world. And Saint Thomas arrived—probably in person—almost to the middle of India, which was the extreme edge of the known Eastern world. How did they do it? What were they made of? What did they build?

People, seeing them, said: "What people they are! Look what they do! How do they live this way?" The method that they used to arrive at the limits of the earth—as Jesus had already told them—was the method of witness. What does it mean to give witness? Witness is a human reality in the total, banal sense of the word—something that we see, we hear, we touch—contained in a normal experience, but which is the vehicle for—carries within itself—something that is no longer "normal," because it makes people stop and ask themselves: "What do these people have?"

This is analogous to that supreme question that everyone asked Jesus, whether they were friends or enemies: "Where do you come from? Who are you?" And these were friends, those friends that walked "in his footsteps" every day at his house. They knew His mother, His father, His closest relatives; they knew everything about Him (just imagine how in tune John and Andrew were with Him). The witness manifested an observable human behavior, the object of experience on the part of anyone who passed by them, but a behavior which aroused *amazement*, that word we use to indicate what is *exceptional* when it happens. They kindled an astonishment; they were different than others. There was a factor that made their normality abnormal. There happened in the normality of their life, in their ordinary behavior—the content of everyone's experience—a factor that no one understood.

This exceptionality within normal behavior is paradoxical, not contradictory—it is therefore not a fantasy or an emotional illusion—it coincides exactly with what Christianity calls a *miracle*. A miracle is a thing that, in its immediate perception, can be very normal, and yet it has within it something that, by its power, calls me back to God. This is explained in the School of Community volume *Why the Church?* when it speaks about the fruits that the Church bears, about the change that the Church brings to human life. [42]

This is a word that struck me because of the discovery it indicated to us at this time: the miracle is a flame from the divine. We all have a particular way we walk in life, a certain mode, with certain limits. But there is a step, a way of walking, that amazes and indicates, reveals, a dignity or an exceptionality of self-awareness. The miracle is the forward movement of the divine footstep within the steps of a human companionship because—and this is, even more acutely, the great beauty of the revelation of the Mystery that has been manifested, of the Father who spoke to us through the mystery of Christ—God chose (here we see the educative aspect that is eminently present in the work of God toward His creature) as His normal method for educating man to His will, in order to make man worthy of Him, the *total familiarity* with man: God chose a total familiarity!

Just think, God was born from the womb of a young girl! If we do not jump up at this, it is because it affirms something about which we no longer think. But in this phrase, in this message, there is the utterly imposing grandeur of God. In life, one can continue to do what one wants, but one will never be able to subtract oneself from the judgment of this truth: God chose to be familiar. If He is familiar, it means that His footsteps go together with mine. As Moses said on Mount Horeb: "If your Presence does not go with us, do not send us up from here" (Exodus 33:15). This would be the most beautiful prayer we Christians could say in the morning.

The forward movement of Jesus's footsteps in the midst of all the footsteps we make during the day, this is the miracle: the miracle is more common than the non-miracle in our days! The events of the life of Saint Riccardo Pampuri are, for example, an exceptional grace. But what grace is this? The grace of God who pushes us to understand that He is familiar! Therefore, the miracle is not something strange: it is something normal! And there is nothing that can fill us with such a unitary feeling—nothing that can make us feel like brothers and sisters—like the fact of this Mystery who is among us and brings among us every day a super-abundant testimony of Himself, the superabundant comfort of a miracle.

This is what surprised me about my mother when I was a young boy. I didn't understand then, but I remember well that my mother, at a certain point, while she was washing the dishes, stopped— there were still a lot of dishes to wash, and she just stopped. As an adult, I now realize that, for an instant, she was praying. Not even the greatest philosophers, Socrates or Plato (our contemporary philosophers are inferior!), could imagine something like this: that a gesture so normal could flourish because of its relationship with the Infinite, as an offering to God. The miracle coincides with the goodness and justice of our life, such that God, making Himself familiar to us, as a method, fills our life with a miracle—first of all turning everything we do into a miracle. This certainty about the presence of the Lord makes us capable of something like this.

Never, at least for me, in all the history of our movement have I awaited the publishing of our monthly magazine, never have I waited to read *Traces* like I do now, because finally *Traces* is getting closer to being what we always desired it to be: the witness of what our people are living. One reads the letters of *Traces* and reads the story of miracles. What if God, as a reward, makes us people who re-echo in the world a figure like Saint Pampuri, who is so unique in his humility! Yes, because what did he do? At the Saint Joseph clinic, he, the doctor, gave a bedpan to a sick person when the nurse forgot to do it. Everyone was struck by a doctor who was better, kinder, humbler, and more of a servant than a nurse.

It is not that you necessarily have to be thinking about these things while doing everything you have to do. If this was a discov-ery for me, a kind of leap forward in front of certain things, after seventy years, it could be that even after sixty you also don't understand anything. However, it's not true: if we are in this companionship, and certain things happen for some, from that moment, they happen for everyone, in everyone. So, we come to the main question, which was—

How can we help each other as an Association to insert ourselves in this historical moment that the movement is living?

How can you be more within this moment of the movement? How can you be closer to it? Pray to Saint Pampuri, but above all to the Virgin Mary. She is truly a great figure. Just think (this morning I thought of this!) that the first word that the Mystery said to man was: "Do not be afraid! *Ne timeas!*" (cf. Genesis 15:1). Do not be afraid! To do what you do, you need to "be not afraid"—if one is afraid, it is impossible for one to stand, but it is also impossible that it even crosses one's mind to stand! If it comes into your mind to stand fast, this means that already you do not fear anymore; fear does not prevail.

Pray to the saints, to the humble and unknown Pampuri (if it wasn't for Adriano Rusconi, literally no one in the world would know Saint Pampuri), pray to the saints to be as aware as possible of the value of what you are and of what you do, because there is no greater value, there is no greater miracle, than a woman and a man who, having no children, pick up a child, maybe one who has been marked by the Lord's cross—pick him up like he was their own child. It's crazy! And, in fact, there is no comparison: it is a miracle! May Mary and the saints make us always more aware of what God has given us to live.

Read the Letter to the Hebrews, chapter 13. "Be open to hospitality," Saint Paul says. I hope you remember this passage: it is a phrase that should be our motto: "Do not neglect to show hospitality to strangers, for thereby some have entertained angels unawares" (Hebrews 13:2). But it's not that they are angels: they are more than angels! They are children of God, part of the mystery of Christ's person. Thus, what through nature would be like the first instinct, to welcome an angel, proves itself true. In fact, I believe that nature favors the rush of the protective instinct toward a child with Down's Syndrome on the part of a woman who has a maternal heart. It is even confirmed scientifically that the affective impulse toward children carrying in themselves the consequences of original sin which affects the whole world, the instinctive feeling that a woman experiences, is more abundant for a child in this condition than in front of a child not affected in this way.

I wanted to tell you to be aware that you are the beating heart of the life of the movement. We would no longer recognize our movement if you were not present. (Not you in the sense of person A, B, or C, but if there was not what you, A, B, and C, do, no matter the awareness you have of it.) That you be more aware of it is a hope that we have for you, because if you are more aware of it, then it shines all the more! It is like seeing someone who goes around in a dark night all lit up. And people are encouraged. People are encouraged, seeing and reading about what you are living.

We think that if the Fraternities—excuse me for using an aspect of our particular method—would help in this: the Fraternities that we are promoting and who do not know what to do when they gather together, they don't know what to say, looking for things to say, looking for things to do, when they should be helping each other to "be" in what they already do, to be aware of what they are doing—my God! Because what they do is what Christ did, is what Christ is doing: they save the world, giving the world the certainty that there is a Father, giving the world evidence, or hope, that there is a life that is the end of everything that happens, that they are loved, that each person is loved, giving the world the spectacle of a real sacrifice, however great or small it is.

For this reason, you should not seek first of all for others to see what you are doing: if they see that you are trying to be seen, they will see less. Instead, if it doesn't matter to you to be seen or not to be seen, but you offer yourselves to the Father, the whole world will see, even without seeing, according to the beautiful phrase of a famous Greek philosopher: "The hidden harmony [the hidden truth] is better than the open."[43]

The Mystery that makes the world is the Father: His method of relationship with His creatures is familiarity; familiarity in the most powerful sense of the word, maternal or paternal. He becomes a presence in our companionship. But this presence has an accent, has a way of walking that astonishes us: the miracle is His specific way of being with us. Thousands of them happen every day. If only we thought about it! So it is through this that the companionship becomes a witness to Him. Because the companionship could not be what it is without the exceptional thing that is a part of it. Be aware: pray to the Virgin Mary and to the saints—we need to ask for this from Saint Pampuri, even before we care for children, mothers, grandchildren, or ourselves—that we may have the awareness of the infinite value of each gesture.[44] Because when as a little boy I saw my mother stop—it seemed like she was doing nothing for half a minute—it was true what our new friend Giovanni Maspes, in that phrase that we have cited a thousand times, said: "the density of the moment." To discover the joy of this way of one's relationship with the world and of one's humanity happens only for the one who has been called to know the Lord. But we have been called in order that through us, He may reach everyone. Hopefully, He will reach everyone before the end of all things!

We have sought to help each other live and to be always more aware of the unity of the "I," which has also become a dimension of catholicity and of the missionary character (the examples of our families who have welcomed Romanian kids with all that comes with it, or fostering people coming out of the former Yugoslavia, are testimonies of this). We have not been able, though, to reach younger families, the youth.

If you are not reaching young families, something is not right.

Should we change something?

Just don't pose it as a problem of quantity or of saying that this one or that one is at fault. You have to speak about it: speak about it to them, involve them, express to them the happiness that certain experiences can give. Writing a letter to *Traces* means making it known to 60,000 people. Someone says: "I should write what happened here, but it is something so normal!" No! The fact that someone says "normal things" in a certain way is not normal! We are all Christians, but only those who are close to us hear us speak more often about the fact that the method with which God deals with us is that of the miracle! The miracle is something obvious, like eating and drinking. Therefore, we need a greater initiative in making things known but not as a problem of management or publicity. If you really love young people, who still must walk the whole road that you have already walked—if you really love them, the first thing for you to say is: "How happy I am doing this!" and not: "Do this, do that, in politics, technology, or work."

I know people who would never be interested in God or in the Church. But they are more seriously interested than the people brought up through this educational effort for more than ten years because they have seen the way one of you does a certain thing: they saw one of you come back with a child from Romania, for example. Because the method with which Jesus moved from that relationship with John and Andrew to the relationship with millions and millions of people in all the world—a method that has created a history that challenges time and space—came through the testimony of certain people: whoever has encountered this testimony has understood that there was something beyond and felt impelled to do something more.

However, the moment that the movement is living is precious because, in forty years, the Lord has never been so good to us. For example, a fundamental aspect of our difficulty is the "division" between us and the world: we are in the world (because we are like everybody else), but what we say and so many things that we do are not of the world: the world does not repeat the *Creed*. There is a way of saying the *Creed* that moves a stranger who has never said it. Anyway, this wall that exists—analogous to the one Saint Paul speaks about between the Jews and the Gentiles (the pagans)—this wall that has always divided what we have said about ourselves, what we have done and are doing, from the world, has in these years begun to break down. For example, in America, it is an astonishing thing: the relativistic American attitude is absolutely impermeable to ours; if you say that something "is," you are considered a fundamentalist; you cannot say "is," you have to say "may be" and then within that "may be," you can do whatever you want. And instead, no! Our most difficult texts, the most alternative ones, are now published by one of the greatest publishing houses in America. This is something that we have been trying to do for twenty years! And this was not born from the good outcome of our attempts. It was born gratuitously: while we were in one sense making an effort, we were also waiting—hidden away, so to speak. I received a letter the other day, signed by the Pope, as a thanksgiving for our Christmas greetings, in which he called us to continue living with passion so that others may know Christ. It is a recognition that is as exceptional as it is familiar.

We have a few other questions.

So, let me repeat, this is the only thing that is important to me: that you pray to the Virgin Mary and to the saints to be always more aware of what you are doing, washing dishes or the kids' clothes (which perhaps, because of their condition, get dirty more often), without getting upset, trying not to get upset because this is self-control that demands the keeping of a certain memory.

And then, build and live well the Fraternity, according to our concept of fraternity: a group of people who live close, or get together, for the sake of holiness. Holiness means the love of being, that is, man's love for God, as Dionysius the Areopagite said. I remember this phrase, which at the beginning, I had us read and repeat as often as possible: "Who could ever speak to us of the love that Christ has for man, overflowing with peace?"[45]

And one may be full of errors. This is the value of our concept of morality, which is born from the "yes" of Peter: not born as an observation of laws, but as the affection for a great Presence that he discovered. "Do you love me?" (John 21:15ff). Saint Peter could be weighed down by errors, buried in them—but he said yes all the same. This is the attachment that identifies our conception of morality. In this sense, Jesus said: "Truly, I say to you, the tax collectors and the harlots go into the kingdom of God before you" (Matthew 21:31). This is not a paradox because He said it! True morality is the recognition of a belonging: "I belong to You, O Lord, whatever I am. Make me different!" "And every one who thus hopes in him purifies himself as he is pure" (1 John 3:3). This is not an indifference, though, but a freedom to set out again. This is the most difficult thing to understand.

Even this is another miracle: that there are people who understand morality completely differently than others, not as laws to observe for a certain balance in society, or of rules to apply, a technique to be used, but as the surprise and the amazed recognition of a Presence that is relevant to my heart, to what my heart desires.

In our experience of hospitality, we always encounter the pain of our children, who are born, who live, who carry signs of a really heavy history, and the pain of our own families, when they face and welcome the fact that these children have not been generated by them, that they are always from other parents who have brought them into the world, and even before this, the pain of the same families when they are not able to have children. So many of us have asked to be helped to be at the level of that original dependence about which you spoke.

Help comes when you live in a Fraternity. The Fraternity is a group of people who get together to understand, to feel, and to live these things. Holiness lies in this: because everyone becomes calmer, they can face things with an equilibrium. I told you this also in 1993 (I always use this comparison): is being a father or mother the same as pushing a fetus out of the womb? No! And if you welcome a fetus made by another woman for two months, four months, five months, and you educate him, you are the mother, in the physiological and ontological sense of the term! And if you do this, even without having the child in the house with you—because your husband does not want to, or because you are afraid and you don't feel up to it, even when you prayed to God—in so far as you know about a poor child who lives in a bad situation, mistreated by a family that is not his, and you offer the whole day, saying in the morning: "Lord, I offer you my day so that you may help that baby," this is an even finer maternity, more "genetic" than any other maternity.

In fact, our mothers, who were Christian mothers, looked at their children like this! My mother was known for being one of the famous (in our town) disciples of a certain priest named Father Amadeo. He was the priest of the girls' association at the parish, criticized by the parish priest, who took him out of the girls' association and confined him to the confessional. And he, after a little disorientation, picked himself up and from the confessional created in the town a stream, a movement, of young women who were always ready; there were about a hundred women, and any time there was a need, he ran to them (even the pastor ran to them). Anyway, my mother always said: "Poor Father Amadeo"; "Poor Father Amadeo gave the blessing"; "Poor Father Amadeo over here, poor Father Amadeo over there." My mother, trained by "Poor Father Amadeo," had lived a beautiful detachment with respect to her children. Because not even a child with Down's Syndrome is yours; he is more yours than another one of your children, in a certain sense; but nothing is ours, everything is Christ's, and Christ is God's.

You said: "Live the Fraternity." I understood this as: "Live among yourselves in a Fraternity," that is, with that fullness of a reciprocal relationship.

Yes, among you if it is possible, but you can also live it with others. It is the way of communicating to others your generosity—and what generosity!—your example, your consolation. Walking with them, you said: "I've done it like this, or like that. Now, you do it! Let's do it together. Let's help each other." Instead, it happens that everyone, in all of Italy, makes fraternities, but they do not understand what the Fraternity really is. I repeat: they look for things to say, for things to repeat, for things to organize. No! We need to look together for what we should love.

I believe that the grace the Lord has given us, the supreme grace, is that of having persuaded ourselves without realizing it—and we do not realize it—of an ascetic method, that is, of a method for walking in time and space, of walking toward our destiny, of a method that is absolutely simple, just like following Him was simple. "What should I do, Teacher, to be on top of things?" "Follow me." Something so simple! Just think about your visit to Romania, to Transylvania. Look at our friend Giorgio: if there is someone who has a need, he helps that person in his need, and if there is the possibility to build something upon that need, he builds it; he tries to build something. To create a society is to build something based on the needs of man. We just need to avoid being presumptuous.

There is a danger that we all risk: after a little, instead of remaining simple in front of a miracle, we say: "I understand; now I'll go ahead on my own."

Instead, the greater you become, the more time that passes, the more you find yourself amazed in front of the face of a young person: for this reason, "death is young." I used to have us sing, in the mountains with GS (when there still wasn't anything called GS), "our youth never passes away," and not "never returns," as the old song used to say.[46] If someone were to ask me: "Who should you thank the most, of the whole movement, in so far as he attempts to live out the message that you brought without understanding what you were saying?" I would respond: the people in Welcoming Families. I have no one to thank more than these, that is, more than you all. But the problem is for God to make you contagious. We need, so to speak, for everyone who lives this hospitality to be hosted by the group they create; we need everyone to participate in a group and to feel truly welcomed by this group (because one can be in a group without being welcomed like the children we foster). So that the laughter of our hearts, which God gave us and for which we are grateful, may tempt other people too!

The most beautiful phrase in this sense (from the Ambrosian liturgy—it does not exist in the Roman liturgy; Saint Ambrose is the genius of mercy, which is why he converted Saint Augustine) is in the *Hexameron*. Saint Ambrose comments on all the days of

Creation. The last line of the last day, he says: "And finally God rested, because He had someone to forgive."[47] Christianity shows itself to be divine only because of phrases like that! Nobody in this world would be capable of saying something like that: it is a miracle. I hope, therefore, that you can encourage, with the way you live the Fraternity among yourselves, others to create one. Because the Fraternity can be made by anyone: the motive for getting together is such that it is below or above any feeling.

We would like to ask if you would come on 17 March to the inauguration of the Santa Rita della Novella house, which is, so to say, a "child" of the Association. It is in Castel Bolognese, on a Sunday.

I promise that I'll come. Thank you, thank you! This is an experience of human closeness. We must try to save this one thing, at every cost: the freedom to be what we are called to be and to educate for this, to be able to communicate this; we must, that is, save the freedom of the Church, because the Church, in the last analysis, is only this: "God with us." The rest is a consequence. Read the thirty-third chapter of Exodus, one of the most beautiful pages in human literature. God is walking away from Moses, hidden in a cloud on Mount Horeb. Moses is there, with his face to the ground, trying to look, and he says: "Lord, stay with us: If your Presence does not go with us, do not send us up from here." Tell me if you can find a more human expression than this! And the Lord says: "I will do the very thing you have asked, because I am pleased with you, and I know you by name. I will walk with you, and you will be my people." Silence. After a little, Moses adds: "Now show me your glory, show me your face." Instead, we always see the back of the Lord, not His face. Because, God responds, "no one may see me and live." We have to be dead to see the face of God: to be alive, we must die. Everyone, instead, slides into the presumption of imagining for himself the face of God, of defining God according to his own imagination and pleasure. It is for this reason that we have entitled the new School of Community text *Alla ricerca del volto umano* [*In Search of the Human Face*] because the human face is the indirect reverberation of the face of God: God is known through what man is.[48] Thank you for what you do.

APPENDICES

The Person, Subject of a Relationship

THE PHENOMENON OF THE man-woman relationship, seen in its existential context from the Christian point of view, leads us to the discussion of these three points:

- The subject, the actor in question, is the *person*;
- This subject is called to carry out a role, a function: the idea of *function* governs the second part of any discourse on Christian marriage;
- Both the person and the function that this subject is called to carry out are immersed in a *social and historical context* that conditions—not only tends to condition, but inevitably conditions—both the self-awareness of the person and the image of his or her function.

The Person

The subject of the conjugal relationship is the person. From this point of view, keeping in mind what Christian anthropology says about this synthetic and supreme value, it is important to stress that because the person is defined by their relationship with destiny, which is God, the phenomenon of matrimony cannot be for its own sake for the man and the woman who enter into it. The idea of the person—the value of the person in the two subjects involved—establishes within the phenomenon of marriage an ultimate position of detachment that permits the true possession of things. But the detachment that permits the true possession of things cannot happen, cannot be fulfilled, if the subject is not already aware of something that is greater than the passing things that interest him. If man finds his ultimate support in something that he has in his hands, he cannot gain any detachment from it, and therefore he cannot possess it; he cannot be free.

In this sense, the idea of the person instills in the heart of things, even the most personal things, the capacity for rising above without which we are not truly owners of what we do. It is perhaps here that we can reintroduce the importance that the ancient word *ascesis* has in the Christian ethical tradition. The word *ascesis* includes everything we have said before about a rising above that lies at the heart of the things that are most precious to us—a rising above that makes possible this detachment, that, in its time, assures that the reality of the relationship with the other is in our hands without gaining control over us.

A corollary. It follows from what we have said that a true respect of man toward woman (and vice versa) can be born—a respect that isn't at the mercy of fleeting feelings (no matter how generous and prudent they may be). Instead, that respect comes from the fact that the other is someone who cannot be reduced to appearance, to reaction, to desire, to pleasure. It is from this respect that we can learn how to refrain from instrumentalizing the other.

That a man may live toward a woman (or vice versa) without instrumentalization is present in Christian discourse precisely as a corollary of the awareness that the other—who is a relationship with God—is a person. Otherwise, according to Christian discourse, it becomes possible to exploit the other. We can see that people's gathering into a society, if conceived outside of the authentic religious fact—therefore of a fact that has a clear sense of God as Person and of the relationship of man with this God—seeks to solve problems through instrumentalization, which attacks at its base every construction between man and woman, just as it does with every relationship between man and man.

The discourse we are highlighting now means that the relationship of a man with a woman, if it does not obey this rising above the self, is not true—it doesn't exist. The relationship between man and woman exists, in the strongest sense of the word, only if it recognizes at its root a factor that is greater than this relationship: without this rising above what one does, what one does is not true, that is, in the philosophical sense, it does not exist.

Function

The concept of function, in Christian terminology, coincides with that of vocation: life, being, is conceived as a personal relationship—one that is conscious and free—with the supreme being, in the form of a dialogue that the image of this relationship implies.

The biblical term "vocation" signifies exactly this: that the person is called, in the work that he takes on, in the commitment that he lives with the other person (man and woman), to carry out a task, that is, a moment, even if it is extremely important, but still a moment, within the total design. Man and woman are called to carry out a task that is contained within the total design of God. Even if it is an extremely privileged task, it still remains a task within the total design of God, a task whose substance is shaped by the totality of the design: its consistency does not lie in itself, it cannot stand on its own, unless it takes its meaning from the total design. From this point of view, man and woman have as an ethical ideal, a dynamic direction, what Jesus Christ said about Himself before dying: "Greater love has no man than this, that a man lay down his life for his friends" (John 15:13). From this point of view, the ideal—that is, the law of this dynamic—is an openness to spend oneself in this task.

Aristotle said that in an ideal there is no measure. If we call the ideal the dynamic law of the function that is entrusted to us, the decision to spend our life in that task represents the height of obedience to that ideal. Therefore, according to Christian discourse, a deep openness to the function serves as a "corrective" for what we discussed before.

The first point affirmed, in fact, that the value of the person transcends the relationship that exists between man and woman. Marriage demands this rising above, without which it crumbles. The man does not exploit the woman, and vice versa, in the measure in which this factor of rising above, this self-awareness as religiosity, exists.

The second thing to underline in regard to function, however, is that the ideal is availability to the task to which we are called, to the vocation that has been given to us, to the commitment that we have made—which brings us back to all the seriousness of the problem with which we are engaged.

Now, the man and the woman have an equal dignity. But their equality implies affirming each other in their difference. An equality that had as its own ideal an identity in the material, quantitative sense of the word would be a huge lie. Equality or identity of two subjects implies their diversity, for which attention to the diversity of the other is, deep down, the fundamental element of respect for the other. Is it not easy for a man to treat a woman, I don't say badly, but to use the woman without thinking about her, according to the affective, physical state of his soul, and vice versa? Clearly, this would not be a healthy way of living out the function that we have been called to live.

There is, though, a necessary instrumentalization that happens in order that the function can be carried out. This function—in a theological discourse, in traditional Catholic morality—is always carried out in two steps: the scope of the man-woman relationship is, in the first place, a mutual help and, in second place, for the procreation and education of children.

Clearly, the means used to help each other mutually is different from the means needed for the second aim. That is, an adequate instrumentation for the second purpose is not enough to save the first as well. However, let us not forget that mutual help, in whatever area, that is, treating each other like human beings and not like animals, implies an unavoidable spiritual factor.

Again, the word *ascesis*, which we used before, comes back in all its importance because a husband cannot try to adapt himself to his wife—how can we give each other help if we do not adapt ourselves?—he cannot adapt himself to his wife (and vice versa) without a control and a dominion over himself, without *ascesis*. It is impossible. But also, for the second aim, it is clear, for example, that the education of a child implies the most serious sacrifice of self, of our own ideas and inclinations, of times when we would like things to go a certain way.

It is precisely in carrying out this task—because, among all the jobs that a man and a woman can be assigned in life, this represents the most personal, one that most deeply touches the awareness that they have of themselves—that man and woman can educate themselves to an openness and availability toward others, toward society. Every openness to society, every social sensitivity, every generous sacrifice for others, but even more acutely, every sensitivity in perceiving the value of society—even in the broad sense of the world, of others—passes, according to Christian discourse, through the education that the marriage relationship creates in the individual, in the subject. In the measure that a married man and woman do not put forth the effort, the necessary *ascesis* for adapting to each other, it is impossible for them to open themselves, to educate themselves, to mature in a sensitivity to others. It would be a fiction, a political-sentimental mask.

The Social Context

The person, in carrying out his or her function, is present within a certain social context. This context inevitably influences the person. The social and historical context is always determined by power, and objective power translates the ideological currents in vogue into terms of social determination, that is, the anthropological and social conception of the prevailing ideologies. We can never support the government unless it seeks to implement the factors of the "natural" order and unless it seeks to increase "value"—every man (unless he is absolutely crazy) always speaks from some conception of value and truth. Now in the measure that the current social context is born from power—which acts to concretize a certain philosophy—it will eventually become unjust toward a phenomenon that is as original as the family—and it is inevitable that it will ultimately become unjust toward the person. This will always tend to exploit the family, because power will always affirm its own goal over the ultimate goal of the family, which is to follow the design of God.

One symptom of this exploitation in the social context in which we live is the attempt to divide the meaning of the life of the parents from that of the children, to divide the family—the parent-child axis. Similarly, earlier social contexts tried to identify the meaning of the face of the children with the will of the parents. In a conformist society, every push to maintain the *status quo* will seek to eliminate the newness that is presented by children; so also, a disputatious society like our own inevitably will tend to "do no harm"—it will say—eliminating the connection between parents and children to liberate the new for the sake of new goals that the society pursues.

I just wanted to mention these three points in the Christian discourse about the family.

The *person*. At the heart of the phenomenon of marriage there is a rising-above that very phenomenon. Because a person is not made for marriage, but for their destiny—for God. Fulfillment, the completion of the person, lies not in marriage but in their end. In this sense, a position of *ascesis* and detachment truly permits the possession of what is made. Not to instrumentalize the other means respecting this prospect that lies beyond the one who is seen, even if that one is seated at the same table. It is through the affirmation of this rising-above, which is at the heart of the phenomenon, that we also live the truth of the very phenomenon. If I take a book and put it close to my eyes, I cannot see it; if I am nervous and in order to possess it, I put it close to my eyes, I do not possess it—I possess it much less, precisely as a book: without this detachment, I do not possess something for what it truly is.

I did not linger here to say what the relationship of matrimony has to do with the destiny of the person. I wanted to say that matrimony is not the ultimate aim either of the man or of the woman. But then, what does marriage mean for the destiny of man and woman? I did not answer this question but moved directly to the second point.

The *function*. Marriage is a function, a vocation to fulfill the design of God. From this point of view, the fundamental attitude is a deep openness to God's design.

Naturally, if the purpose of this relationship demands a stability that at a certain point is no longer pleasing to the man and the woman engaged in this "game," the man and the woman must sacrifice themselves to this purpose, to the necessities of the purpose, to the demands that the purpose brings forth. Herein lies the Church's whole teaching on divorce.

I have mentioned that respect for difference is the only way to experience equality between the two and the right that the man and the woman have to the tools that will help them pursue their goal (think, for example, how the lack of education, illiteracy, or unemployment can be a hindrance to pursuing their goal or how a certain type of urban planning can gravely harm the right that a man and woman have to carry out their purpose, etc.).

Anyway, according to the conception of the Church, the development in man of a true sensibility and availability to the needs of the world is nothing other than the manifestation of an *ascesis*, of an effort, of a generosity, with which he lives the affective event. The modality with which a man lives the affective event is the same modality with which, in the end, he carries himself toward the world.

And lastly, the value of the *social context*. While recognizing the good that the social context accomplishes for man and woman and for their relationship—with the help that this really gives to the phenomenon of the family, exalting one or the other of the factors necessary to the well-being of the family—Christian discourse must realistically underline the impossibility of the social context (always, in the whole of history) to fully respect the natural value of the family. It is impossible that the social context can respect the fact that the family comes before it: if the family comes before the social context, the social context has to respect it. Instead, in the whole conception in vogue today, dominated by a secular culture, the priority of the family is by no means recognized (just think here about all the problems of religious education, as the Church has always maintained and the Second Vatican Council renewed in its document *Gravissimum educationis*).[49] Even so, many priests and religious, and so many of those who work at private schools, are tranquilly, for all I know, toeing the secular line in regard to education, of the right to education and to certain modes of education.

The social context will always tend to see the family as part of itself, as its own property. The division that exists within the family seems to be the most unrelenting symptom of this disproportion and of this contradiction between society and family. In this sense, the nineteenth chapter of Saint Matthew recalls a very interesting phrase of Christ (it is a phrase that refers to the problem of the vocation to virginity and to the problem of being free from riches): "With men this is impossible, but with God all things are possible" (Matthew 19:26). This means the Church—the Church not in an abstract sense, the Church in the concrete, the Church which emerges as a community in a setting of men and women who are married—represents a unique corrective or a place of defense from attack that, beyond any of its intentions, the whole social context always makes against families, a recovery of the strength of its original right.

A final "nota bene." What I am about to say is not very popular—and even rather unpopular—but it belongs to the logic of the discourse. Because morality is identical to rationality, to reasonableness, and because reasonableness of life is established from the relationship between what one does and the final end, if my expression makes me stretch forth toward my destiny, toward my end, in this exact measure, it is good—otherwise it is a lack, a shortcoming. So, the relationship between man and woman, as the total involvement of two beings, has a determinate purpose, of which at least its most resounding and impressive aspect is the procreation and education of children.

If we can imagine a nature that did not need to procreate, the separation and distinction of the sexes would be absurd. However, the essence is that the first meaning of the distinction is procreation. Unless the relationship between man and woman has the aim of a sexual commitment, the affectivity between the two does not lead to the issue of sexuality. But the complete commitment of the couple is for a determined purpose. Even before any formal commitment, according to the whole dimension of marriage, before a definitive commitment, which the purpose of marriage demands, it is assumed by the man and woman that this commitment is a true path, but it cannot claim to be a definitive commitment.

Let us pose the case of two who are engaged for eight years, and then, at a certain point, the man falls in love with another. It was the last thing he would have thought of up until two months ago. After eight faithful and tranquil years, for two months, it has been out of order: the first to be full of pain, in fact, is the man, and he does not know what to do; he is desperate. It is clear that he is not obligated to get married because the commitment was not definitive. For the Church, this definiteness of a will expressed objectively has an extreme importance. The definiteness of the will, the full act of the will, should be objectively expressed, and this objectivization of this expression of the will is "in front of the community," of society. Without these two connotations, the will is not yet fulfilled. Therefore, we cannot oblige anyone to get married in that situation. Analogously, this man did not yet have the right to a total commitment with his girlfriend.

I chose these things in a fragmentary way, but I chose the ones that seemed the catalysts of all the problems. All the problems that can be born in a discussion about the man-woman relationship, of whatever nature, seem to collapse into these three points: the person, the function, and the social context.

Culture of Life and Culture of Death

> Because God did not make death, and he does not delight
> in the death of the living.
>
> —WISDOM 1:13

TODAY'S MAN, LIKE THE man of yesterday and of tomorrow,
belongs to the Mystery that made him through a thousand smaller
circumstances, those that are welcomed and consciously chosen as
well as those which arise unconsciously. The word that God gave
to man as a light to judge his action at the deepest level, where
those actions are born, is in the Bible, open to the understanding
of everyone.

In the Book of Wisdom, the culture of life is opposed to the
culture of death:

> Because God did not make death, and he does not de-
> light in the death of the living. For he created all things
> that they might exist, and the generative forces of the
> world are wholesome, and there is no destructive poison
> in them; and the dominion of Hades is not on earth. For
> righteousness is immortal (Wisdom 1:13-15).

This is the promise with which God has created us: and this
is justice.

Even so, the Book of Wisdom continues:

But ungodly men by their words and deeds summoned death; considering him a friend, they pined away, and they made a covenant with him, because they are fit to belong to his party. For they reasoned unsoundly, saying to themselves, "Short and sorrowful is our life, and there is no remedy when a man comes to his end, and no one has been known to return from Hades. Because we were born by mere chance, and hereafter we shall be as though we had never been; because the breath in our nostrils is smoke, and reason is a spark kindled by the beating of our hearts. When it is extinguished, the body will turn to ashes, and the spirit will dissolve like empty air. Our name will be forgotten in time, and no one will remember our works; our life will pass away like the traces of a cloud, and be scattered like mist that is chased by the rays of the sun and overcome by its heat. For our allotted time is the passing of a shadow, and there is no return from our death, because it is sealed up and no one turns back" (Wisdom 1:16–2:5).

As always, the biblical text is a great prophecy thrown out over the life of man. And perhaps these words apply as never before in our tragic time.

In his encyclical dedicated to the Gospel of Life, John Paul II writes:

The Gospel of life, proclaimed in the beginning when man was created in the image of God for a destiny of full and perfect life is contradicted by the painful experience of death which enters the world and casts its shadow of meaninglessness over man's entire existence. Death came into the world as a result of the devil's envy and the sin of our first parents. And death entered it in a violent way.[50]

For men and women in our age, reality—things, people, desires, projects—acquires in this way the character of the frightful appearance described in the Book of Wisdom. Everything seems to bear the common name of nothingness. And everything seems to be dragged down into this vortex that makes us say: "Our existence is like a passing shadow." How terrible is that human attitude that throws the blame on an absolute, total negativity, without the possibility of remedy!

But this attitude is not in accordance with the nature of man—it is rather the outcome of a disloyalty, the fruit of the insinuation of an extraneous factor in human life against how God originally planned and created it. Man, in fact, was not born as negativity but as a positive promise. The babies that exit their mother's womb, from the first instant, cry out with desire for life that is the stuff of their identity, and only with time does an incorrect education weaken this original structure, introducing the doubt that everything is meaningless. Doubt as a starting point toward reality cannot be the foundation of a personal existence because it does not correspond to anything in reality.

The words of the Book of Wisdom, it seems to me, help us understand the theme that has been assigned to us—"Culture of life and culture of death"—because they are a judgment on the mentality that governs our day (consciously or not), that governs the life of people, even many of those who call themselves Christians.

Death dominates the common sentiment, extending over everything the veil of appearance, which lasts an instant and then disappears like snow in the sun. And this negativity leads us to exalt the passing instant of momentary satisfaction because everything else has no hope of lasting.

For this reason, Wisdom pursues its description of the attitude of men who are so reduced in their humanity:

> Come, therefore, let us enjoy the good things that exist, and make use of the creation to the full as in youth. Let us take our fill of costly wine and perfumes, and let no flower of spring pass by us. Let us crown ourselves with rosebuds before they wither. Let none of us fail to share in our revelry, everywhere let us leave signs of enjoyment, because this is our portion, and this our lot. Let us oppress the righteous poor man; let us not spare the widow nor regard the gray hairs of the aged. But let our might be our law of right, for what is weak proves

itself to be useless. Let us lie in wait for the righteous man, because he is inconvenient to us and opposes our actions; he reproaches us for sins against the law, and accuses us of sins against our training. He professes to have knowledge of God, and calls himself a child of the Lord. He became to us a reproof of our thoughts; the very sight of him is a burden to us, because his manner of life is unlike that of others, and his ways are strange. We are considered by him as something base, and he avoids our ways as unclean; he calls the last end of the righteous happy, and boasts that God is his father. Let us see if his words are true, and let us test what will happen at the end of his life (Wisdom 2:6-17).

Here is the whole world as we know it—at least for the last few centuries: an exaltation of appearances as the only reason to live; a hostility toward the one who in any way says that the consistence of things is elsewhere and that the reality which makes itself evident in experience is something else.

Like the just man in the biblical story, even we today have been called to live a responsibility toward our fellow men and women who are assaulted by a kind of toxic cloud that makes our reason go astray and obscures our vision. And the first victim of this general poisoning is the family, that elementary level of friendship between man and woman that has a particular role assigned to it: the collaboration with God in extending life on the Earth through the procreation of children.

Now, at what level is the problem of a culture of life located? To help ourselves respond, we must look at our elementary experience, to which the Church responds with the announcement of Christ dead and risen, and thus alive for all of history until eternity.

Life as Mission

The point of departure for building up a culture of life is the recognition of life as a mission. Jesus says: "I came that they may have life, and have it abundantly" (John 10:10). The goal of life that God gives is something that seems to be annulled by death.

We have a Christian vocation. This comes to us well before our being man or woman: "For as many of you as were baptized into Christ have put on Christ. There is neither Jew nor Greek, there is neither slave nor free, there is neither male nor female; for you are all one in Christ Jesus" (Galatians 3:27-28). There is a profound principle that gives quite a different meaning to the Christian vocation, however gracious and at least initially so fascinating as the affective relationship is between man and woman—a principle that, being unique, can guarantee continuity and faithfulness in time.

This is literally true: without the awareness expressed by Saint Paul, the worldly mentality—we could also call it the modern mentality, our looking at things with the eyes of flesh, our seeing things as every natural eye would see them—see divorce as an ideal of humanity and compassion because a deep and true relationship is impossible. In fact, what makes continuity possible is not the love of the man and the woman, but the love of the man and the woman which is made possible by the love of another thing. We have been touched in the depths of our being by this seed: this gesture is called Baptism, this sign that is otherwise insignificant, with which Christ has loved us, has touched us, and chosen us.

For what has He chosen us and why? Because we are more coherent or better than others? No. "As the Father has sent me, so I send you." Life as mission is the only exhaustive definition of life in Jesus because the awareness of our life as mission exhausts our self-awareness and the value of all that is born from us. If we do not start out from this, we will put something else in first place, something formed by the worldly sense of existence: success, the material care for children, hospitality. But these things the pagans also do, so there would be no need to be Christian to practice these things.

What is mission? For what reason has the Mystery to which we belong sent us? John Paul II reminds us of it: "When he presents the heart of his redemptive mission, Jesus says: 'I came that they may have life, and have it abundantly.'"[51] And the seventeenth chapter of John's Gospel specifies: "And this is eternal life, that they know thee the only true God, and Jesus Christ whom thou hast sent" (John 17:3). Because: "All things are yours . . . the world or life or death or the present or the future—all are yours, and you are of Christ, and Christ is of God" (cf. 1 Corinthians 3:21-23). The papal encyclical continues: "To proclaim Jesus is itself to proclaim life. For Jesus is 'the word of life' (1 John 1:1). In him 'life was made manifest' (1 John 1:2); he himself is 'the eternal life which was with the Father and was made manifest to us' (1 John 1:2). This Gospel of Life is identical to Jesus himself."[52]

Therefore, the point of departure is the conversion of each person to Christ, the liberation of each person, so that life becomes a duty to announce Christ ever more maturely and consciously. Even the liturgy of marriage says so: God gives children so that they may be regenerated in Christ (according to the Ambrosian rite).[53]

Here, then, is the point of departure: life as a mission. The heart of everybody makes everything flow from this, but not in an automatic way, because there is always and everywhere the involvement of freedom, the modality with which God wants to be in relationship with His creature. In any case, from this beginning, the possibility of a culture of life takes flesh, a culture that invests every aspect of existence and of society. The family is for a man and a woman the daily and continual beginning of a new society. This is the structure of the relationship that most humanly testifies to what makes mission possible: the sacrament of Baptism. Every other sacrament is the consequence of this. Marriage has this precise sense: to complete the face of the missionary subject. And the first mission is between the wife and the husband, or better, the first mission is within ourselves. We often fall into the error of thinking that just living together will generate communion, while it is the mystery of Christ in us that generates communion.

Education

The family fulfills its vocation through the education of children because the goal is not simply to procreate but to educate to the meaning of life. The beginning of our movement quickly formulated a song expressive of this: "Poor is the voice of a man who does not exist; such is our voice if it does not have a reason . . . all of life begs for eternity."

A fruit and symptom of this missionary consciousness, and therefore also of the communion that unites man and woman, is the education of children. Our babies grow up observing how we adults live. Therefore, to educate children means to make them participate in the reality of the communion of the man and woman who gave them life.

> It is above all in educating children that the family fulfils its mission to proclaim the Gospel of life. By word and example, in the daily round of relations and choices, and through concrete actions and signs, parents lead their children to authentic freedom, actualized in the sincere gift of self, and they cultivate in them respect for others, a sense of justice, cordial openness, dialogue, generous service, solidarity and all the other values which help people to live life as a gift. In raising children Christian parents must be concerned about their children's faith and help them to fulfil the vocation God has given them.[54]

It is not as obvious as it might seem that education is taken seriously in a family that lives in today's climate. The theologian Jungmann defined education as what helps another enter into the whole of reality, but this requires a richness of concerns that today's climate tends to discourage so that the life of adults can be as quiet as possible. Moreover, the current climate has an attitude that tranquilly justifies everything, eliminating even the distinction between good and evil.

Therefore, if on one side it seems evident that the family is the first setting for education (this, in fact, is the first dynamic structure in which nature actualizes its capacity for generation and development), on the other side it is not so taken for granted that the educative concern guides the presence and action of parents. In the confusion of values that characterizes the world, how to help children "grow up" from the human point of view has become secondary with respect to other concerns: health, preparation to get a good position at work and in society.

However, it must be said that no climate or moment of history can avoid what each person by nature carries within himself, and thus it can never abolish the anxieties and demands that vibrate in the heart of the person, his nature created by God.

The most important thing, the necessary thing for education, is also the first thing that gets lost today; at one point, the social climate allowed it to remain, even in an unconscious way, but the climate today rips it up. To understand what this thing is that's so necessary for education, let's imagine a mother who goes into the bedroom in the morning to wake up her baby. Suppose that, in a particularly fortunate moment, she stops two meters from the bed and watches her child sleep—the one who came out of her, who did not exist before—and, almost ignoring the fact that her child belongs to her, she thinks: "What is waiting for my child in life; what will he encounter?" and then: "This little one has a destiny; otherwise it would have been unjust and useless to bring him to birth because to bring him into the world means exposing him to the possibility of the greatest difficulties."

It is a human sentiment that this baby belongs to you, mother, but he is not yours. He has his *own* destiny! In Christian terms, it is said, with a very pregnant term, that he has his own vocation—that is, he has been called by Someone who is not you, and this Someone calls him to a goal, to an end that is not you, father and mother. Here is the guarantee of a culture of life, that is, of the positive development of a promise with which we have been drawn into existence.

The first condition to be able to educate a human creature—children, springtime for the family and for society—is that there be a sense of detachment, of respect, this sense of fear and trembling for the Mystery which is within that creature, who is so much yours and yet not yours. Without this detachment, how can a father or mother respect and help the footsteps of a path that they cannot fix, not even for themselves? Father and mother end up inevitably fulfilling the terrible prophecy of the Book of Wisdom, falling into a possessiveness of the child that, while it tries to take hold of him, suffocates him.

On the contrary, the detachment of which we are speaking is like the feeling of not being able to exhaust the relationship with the child while you hold him in your arms, taking him by the hand and enjoining on him what to us adults seems most just, most true, and most adapted to him. It is a real detachment. But there is no unity with our own child deeper than that lived with a father and a mother who seek to guide their child while keeping always before their eyes this tremendous and mysterious thing that is the destiny of that child, having always before their eyes this thought: that he is a being in relationship with Someone who is far greater than us, toward whom I must accompany this child and toward whom he will walk by using, hour by hour, the things and events in which he will be engaged. Therefore, I must help him to use things, to make him take life as much as possible in such a way that his path, moment by moment, is stretched out toward destiny. Otherwise, it would have been useless and unjust to have generated him, because then it would be useless to live; those impious people of whom the Bible speaks would be right!

People are educated if they foster within themselves the expansion of an ideal, an ideal that is something ultimate, greater than themselves, for which everything that they do is not done for themselves alone. This is the abolition of egoism and the beginning of a defense of life as a path toward the destiny prepared by God for each one of us.

The Formation of a People

The family does not participate in the culture of life by itself but together with others. By gathering in unity with these others, their expansion constitutes the movement of the Christian people.

We have said that the family is fundamental as an educative factor. We must at this point add, though, that the family's power is brief and above all fragile. It is like a home, like a room continually struck by lightning. The family is now assaulted by such social forces that it cannot, in any way, save its educative capacity by itself. In truth, this is not only true for our day. I remember the novel *The Garden of the Finzi-Continis*: the ideal of that family was that of living safe within the walls of a great garden, so self-sufficient as to seem autonomous, but an accidental change of fortune overwhelms it.[55]

It is neither intelligent nor sincere to want to educate solely through the instrument of the family. This has always been true, but in our time, it assumes a value of exceptional importance, such that if at one time the resistance of the family or its influence on its children could be valued at seventy percent, now it can only be valued at five percent.

But what does the family do in front of the force of a society that has access to the family through television? What does the family do in front of a school where a teacher can say whatever he likes and whatever seems good to him, sabotaging the conscience of the child however he likes (and this action is systematic)? What does the family do in front of all the advertisements? A family cannot resist by itself.

Therefore, the family's concern for education is intelligent and human in the measure that it determines to come out from its comfort zone and establish relationships that create a social network that opposes itself to the dominant social network. The proper place for this is the communion of the Church. In his encyclical *Mater et Magistra*, John XXIII indicated the freedom of association as one of the ten fundamental human rights. John Paul II also writes: "We have been sent as a people. Everyone has an obligation to be at the service of life."[56]

Having children to educate is the greatest opportunity that God gives to reawaken our faith. There is a moment of life when, maybe through the example of others or mobilized by a sense of impotence in front of a certain duty, faith appears as something interesting not only for eternity but also for this life. This is how a light breaks on the horizon of our life like the dawn of a new day.

"The Gospel of life is for the whole of human society. To be actively pro-life is to contribute to the renewal of society through the promotion of the common good."[57] One begins to perceive a meaning in living, a taste for life, a usefulness in life, that for each person insinuates a new perspective within the modern context that seems inevitably destined to death, that is, to nothingness. But "God did not make death, and he does not delight in the death of the living. For he created all things that they might exist" (Wisdom 1:13-14). This is the great promise that the Christian announcement carries forth, definitively and securely, by the energy of the risen Christ who has conquered and conquers the world.

> The Gospel of life is not simply a reflection, however new and profound, on human life. Nor is it merely a commandment aimed at raising awareness and bringing about significant changes in society. Still less is it an illusory promise of a better future. The Gospel of life is something concrete and personal, for it consists in the proclamation of the very person of Jesus.[58]

This is how the Gospel of life becomes a culture of life, according to the expression of John Paul II: "A faith that does not become culture is not fully accepted, not entirely thought out, not faithfully lived."[59]

The Story of a Work

Welcoming Families

Edited by
CARLA MASSARI

Birth and Development

The Beginnings: Building Places of Friendship

IN A STORY, THE BEGINNING always constitutes a distinctive moment: when freshness of intuition and intensity of mobilization arise in response to the originating circumstance.

The event at the origin of Welcoming Families was a request for an opinion about adoption (for which the City of Milan was preparing a regulation) made by city council member Giuseppe Zola to a group of families who lived an experience of hospitality and to those workers who were involved with them. But at a deeper, more objective level lay the fact that these families—thanks to the education that they received in the ecclesial movement Communion and Liberation—lived the same experience (even if separately), the same ideas, and undertook the same labors in opening their homes to the needs they encountered.

Finding each other working together, they understood that a stable friendship "constitutes a place of discussion and of expansion for our own humanity that institutions cannot give" and a "service for all the other families."

So, on May 18, 1982, the "Welcoming Families Association" was born, which proposed to enhance and support, through the formation of families, hospitality to minors and adults in difficulty—and to spread the value of that work. The people who helped to found this association were Alda Vanoni De Carli, Lia Sanicola, Carla Bagattini Massari, Daniela Fumagalli, Donata Ferrari Carmo, Giuseppe Albetti, Mario Zarpellon, Cesare Mozzanica, Claudio Monaco, and Bruno Marcotti.

The National Conventions: Learning the Reasons

Soon another opportunity presented itself. If the first had been to create places of friendship and dialogue, the next step—almost a natural consequence of the first—was the cultural deepening of the experience, so that the richness which many were living could become more conscious and more communicable, and thus more imitable.

In 1984, a seminar in four lessons was organized in collaboration with the San Carlo Cultural Center (now called The Cultural Center of Milan): "For a Culture of Welcome," featuring speakers such as Father Angelo Scola[60] and Bishop Francis Cox, of the Pontifical Council for the Family.

In 1985, the first national conference of the Association took place: "Hospitality: The Face of Gratuitousness," with remarks by Father Luigi Giussani, Professor of Moral Theology and founder of Communion and Liberation, and by Rocco Buttiglione, Professor of Philosophical Anthropology, and by a few of the families who spoke about their personal experiences.

This first conference, and in particular the contribution by Father Giussani, constituted a point of decisive growth: an occasion to learn the truest reasons, the greatest and thus the most human reasons for our gesture of hospitality—an occasion to give witness to the forms of a new society.

Over the years, the guidance of Father Giussani would be faithfully sought out and would concretize itself, whether in individual encounters with some of our leaders or in encounters with all the members of the governing board. The content of these encounters, some of which are published in this volume, would be the object of a permanent study on the part of all the groups of the Association. The teachings of Father Giussani, such as the specific indications that emerged from them, would thus constitute the backbone of a method for our work.

The Birth of the Houses: The Form of Desire

For some families, the experience of hospitality assumed a fuller, more structured form: they would move to renovated farmhouses to welcome more children and adults. Even in form, the choice for hospitality had become all-encompassing.

In 1980, before the Association was born, Mario Zarpellon (who would later be one of the founding members of the Association), together with his wife Gina and their family, opened a house of hospitality in Baruccana di Seveso (Milan).

Mario and Gina labored for years to create a story of friendship and to cause the awareness of their experience to grow through their testimonies and a paternity full of warmth toward everything they drew near. Now, because of their advanced age, Mario and Gina have left the house at Seveso, donating it to the Grassi Foundation, which hosts terminally ill patients.

So also, Laura and Claudio, went to live in a large house in 1987 in Merate (Lecco) and, starting from the total dedication with which they welcomed their adoptive children in gravely difficult situations, they opened their house to welcome mothers who were addicted to drugs.

A National Reality and Beyond

Whether it is a particular circumstance, the maturity of awareness on the part of some, the capacity for paternity and for guiding others, or all these things together, they have favored, throughout the history of the Association, the awareness of the need for renewal—as a sign of gratitude for the richness being lived and as energy for a more resolute path.

In the 1990s, a number of regional groups became more consistent, and their mutual sharing enabled them to take on greater responsibility. The multiplicity of experiences—which were characterized also in relation to different local, social, and institutional realities—became an occasion for unity in the search for the truth of experience.

Today the Association is present in all the regions of Italy. It has its national headquarters in Milan and is formally constituted in Abruzzo, Emilia Romagna, Liguria, Veneto, and Sardinia. Since 1989, it has spread to Switzerland and in 2001 was established in Spain.

Hospitality without Borders

In the 1990s, in response to the dramatic reality of countries marked by war or by material and moral poverty, the Association committed itself to an important work of temporary hospitality in Italy or of aid to the home countries, with a particular focus on Lebanese, Romanian, and Croatian children.

In 1994, the dramatic situation of Croatian children, who were orphans and refugees, put the question to the leaders of the Association: What should we do? In Italy, it was not possible to host children due to political and bureaucratic difficulties. And so, the idea of helping families in the place where they were began to take shape.

In Zagreb, Zara, and Dubrovnik, Croatian families were helped to welcome refugee children, or handicapped children, or refugee families in grave difficulty. Thus, a kind of foster care by proxy took place: for four years, 300 Italian families were paired up with 300 Croatian families who were sustained by a monthly contribution. "But we were not limited to economic aid: for four years"—recalls Marco—"we went to Croatia every two months to meet families and leaders of local associations who had said yes to the initiative."

In 1997, close to 400 Croatian kids, already known through the initiative of helping families (foster care by proxy), joined a vacation alongside families from Verona and Forli.

In the following years, Italian families in the Association would host different groups of students and adults coming from the East (Russia, Ukraine, Kazakhstan, etc.).

The Work

The Association, over the years, became, above all, a companionship in work—a way of always delving more deeply into the source of its own experience in order to make it more useful. This work remained open to contributions from any source, but first from the paternal guidance of Father Giussani, the teaching of the Church, the experience of the families, and the participation of various disciplines.

In the difficult task of judging the various experiences of the Association, nothing was left out: from how to tell adoptive children about their history to the relationship with social workers.

For many years, the Association has focused on adoption and foster care, and more recently on hospitality for the elderly and children with disabilities.

Adoption

As for adoption, the conference of 1988—"At the Heart of Adoption"—signaled a meaningful step for the Association. Starting in 1991, the number of couples involved grew substantially, and different topics were developed through a dialogue between families and conversations with experts: from couples who struggled with infertility to a deeper knowledge of the situations of abandoned children, from the path of the couples working toward adoption to the school problems of adopted children. The fruit of this work was the publication of a collection of twenty-two pamphlets; over the years, thousands of copies have been circulated.

Since 1993, in order to help those who desire to give themselves to adoption, the experience of "mini-courses" began—cycles of four meetings for small groups of couples guided and accompanied by families who already live the experience of adoption, in the sometimes daunting work of discerning what they truly want.

Foster Care

For those engaging in foster care, the need to be supported by a companionship is fundamental, especially in the face of the temptation to reduce the experience to a "professionalization" of the families.[61]

This friendship allows a family that welcomes a child who is not of their own to live a positive experience so that they may learn a more human gaze, richer in goodwill and in affection between the parents themselves and toward their children.

Over the years, the Association, in order to offer its own contribution of reflection and experience, has organized public meetings and seminars about the topic of fostering in Milan and in other Italian cities.

Furthermore, there a collaboration with social services and other local organizations has developed, whether to help foster families to live the collaborative work of intervention that foster care requires, or to advise families about services for the children in need of welcoming.

The Elderly

For some families the need has an unavoidable proximity: an elderly family member or a disabled child. Thus, we began to work on these experiences of hospitality.

In Milan, in March 1995, a small group of people began to help each other in the experience of hospitality for their own elderly parents, recalling the reasons for this and in dialogue with experts in the field.

In 1996, with the "Simeon Project," a series of meetings were offered on welcoming the elderly with an ongoing consultation service for families of elderly people. In Milan, more than a hundred families were involved in this project, while in other cities a similar experience took shape.

"The Friends of Giovanni"

In 1997, Giovanni was born with Down's Syndrome; his parents met other families with disabled children, and together they sought to help each other understand the adequate reasons to live with hope in this circumstance: a merely pragmatic approach to the problem of handicaps was not sufficient.

"To find ourselves at forty-five years of age beginning from scratch with a child who has problems is not easy. We are asked to have a different gaze, to pray to God, for ourselves and for our children," Tiziana witnesses. Thus, starting in 1998, "The Friends of Giovanni" began to meet once a month and eventually asked to be a part of the Association in order to share the work and friendship that sustains the hospitality of a child, whether he is sick or healthy, young or old.

Today close to thirty families meet up in Milan, among them also families who have adopted children with handicaps. In 2002, between May and June, they organized four public meetings on the topic "Disability, a World to Discover" to face the problem of insertion into the world of school and work, but also the relationship between parents and a child who does not belong to the normal framework.

A Story that Continues

Pilgrimages: Asking to be More Aware

In a meeting with the Board of the Association, Father Giussani said: "Pray to the Mother of God and to the saints to be more aware of what you do. That you may be more conscious is our prayer for you, because if you are more aware, you shine all the more! It is like seeing someone who goes around by night all lit up. And everyone is encouraged."

Even in a gesture of hospitality, the opening up of our home, looking at children or at a spouse can be marred by distraction, by taking things for granted. So we need to pray for the awareness of this gesture and thus the awareness that Christ is present in that face, in that body, becoming a joy for ourselves and consolation for others.

In order to sustain this question in ourselves, every year since 1996, the Association has begun with a simple and essential gesture: the pilgrimage. Thus, in different places but at the same time and in a common way, the regional groups go on pilgrimage to a Marian shrine.

The Exhibit: Testifying to the Fascination of an Experience

A deeper awareness of the gesture of hospitality generates a responsibility to give witness, that is, "made a sign of a newness that like a wave spreads from family to family, from the closest family to the most distant, in a movement that is the beginning of a more human society because it is made of people who are passionate for the destiny of man."[62]

Throughout our history, there have been numerous moments of witness, among which is the participation in public discussions at the "Meeting for Friendship Among People" in Rimini.

One exhibit, "The Possible Home," stands out. Created and promoted by Welcoming Families for the Meeting in 2002, it gave witness to the newness that has invaded the life of many families, the fascination of an experience that seemingly exceeds its own limits, the positivity of the greater life that comes from the sacrifice that this work requires. The exhibit was an occasion to let this witness reach an even larger audience and to propose to everyone that hospitality can be a normal dimension of family life.

Seminars: Responsibility for a Work

Over the years, there have been periodic seminars on the work for the leaders of the whole Association, including those in Spain and Switzerland. The themes have touched on the problems and methods for welcoming others into a family, the building up of a new society, and lastly, hospitality and education: hospitality as an educational experience first of all for those who welcome, and education as attention given to those whom we welcome.

The seminars constitute an important moment of real unity among those who direct this work, but also an important moment of cultural deepening for the whole experience of the Association, beyond and through the specific themes about various forms of hospitality.

From the beginning, the Association has favored the encounter between the need and the person who can welcome it, without ceasing to educate to the necessity of being in front of what you encounter, to the provocation that reality makes, and without ceasing to offer the possibility of experiencing small gestures of hospitality as well.

A Companionship on a Journey: Developments from 2002 to 2012

A first look in retrospect on these ten years, even before naming the numerous initiatives that have been formed, captures the reality of a life. It is the life of men and women, that is, normal families who with freedom have said yes to hospitality and testify to a gratitude for the human beauty of the experience they have had. And to the children, who also carry signs of a difficult history, now let shine through their gazes the serenity of those who have been saved after a storm.

Welcoming Families is a network of friends which sustains families and evokes in them an unexpected capacity to become protagonists. The path of these ten years of the Association has been guided by three foci: education, companionship, and development.

Our first commitment has been to education, which has brought to the center the truth of the person and the family.

The focus has been on the family as a place of meaningful relationships and of reciprocal belonging and *not* primarily a pragmatic instrument to resolve problems of assistance. Thus, the attention is placed on what always becomes more mature in the awareness of what it means to be a family, of what it means to be welcomed and to welcome.

Within this commitment to education, the annual seminars occupy a particular place: these constitute a decisive moment for the path of the whole Association. These are occasions either to take note of the reasons behind our experience and of reciprocal testimony, or of understanding the socio-cultural and legislative context in which we are situated.

In this work, the Association has been sustained by the invaluable contributions of guides, including Father Julián Carrón, Bishop Massimo Camisasca, Cardinal Angelo Scola, Cardinal Carlo Caffarra, Bernhard Scholz, President of the Companionship of Works, and Monica Poletto, President of the Social Works of the Companionship of Works.

The companionship among the families has been more than a network; rather, it has been a true friendship, made up not only of concrete help but also a human accompaniment in the verification of an experience. The goal has been the possibility of "holding on" for the family who welcomes: a family by itself, without a companionship, navigates with difficulty the challenge that the experience of hospitality puts in front of us.

Furthermore, in these last years, precisely the companionship among families, even for enlarging this network, has allowed for a development of topics connected to foster care and adoption and, above all, has assumed the dimension of a welcoming people, capable of giving testimony to a more human way of facing relationships and of encountering needs.

Certain events escape our plans or projections, however dutiful and intelligent. These facts need to be looked at, guided, and accompanied with gratitude by those who understand that the work of Welcoming Families exceeds our capacity and still happens in spite of the limits of each of us. These developments include:

- Welcoming Families received official recognition by the government of Italy as an Association for Social Promotion.

- The Association expanded to other countries, including Spain, Romania, Lithuania, Brazil, and Argentina.

- The number of families who follow the "Friends of Giovanni"—present in many cities—continued to grow. These families welcome children with disabilities and are sustained in a friendship, made up of work, of moments of shared life, and of vacations.

- Some families who already participated in the life of the Association have enlarged their availability to the point of opening a "house of hospitality." It happened in Verona, Chiavari, Genova, Verrucchio, Mornago, and Madrid.

An Experience Matures: The Last Ten Years

In the last ten years, the Association has seen the development of its work and mission and has strengthened its public presence.

On the thirtieth anniversary of the foundation, October 10, 2012, more than 1,500 members participated in an audience with Pope Benedict XVI. It was a pilgrimage that witnessed to their gratitude for the experience they had been given and for a story that was born from a Christianity lived within Communion and Liberation.

The Association was enriched in 2013 by another reality, "Homes for Welcome." It is a network of family homes born within Welcoming Families which shares its aims and methods. This new Association is an important support for the more structured aspects of hospitality, through courses of formation that involve not only families, but also educators, volunteers, and social workers.

To accompany in a more precise way the experience of families and to appreciate their personal and social significance—these were the aims more recently in forming the Adoption Network and the Foster Network within Welcoming Families, coordinated at the national level by groups that, in various locations where the Association is present, gather together families that adopt and foster.

The public presence of the Association over the years has grown considerably with an intensive participation at the directive council of the Forum of Family Associations—an organization that gathers Catholic entities in Italy engaged at various levels with the family—with contributions on various occasions at national institutions.

The collaboration with other associations and communities has intensified and given life to an experience rich in fruit: an example is the "Children of Hope" project. Starting in 2015, the friendship between Welcoming Families and the Orthodox communities of Milan and Kiev has offered 7-12 year old Ukrainian children a period of calm in the summer for them with their families, refugees to Kiev from areas already in conflict.

In early 2022, with the outbreak of war in Ukraine and the wave of refugees from the country, Welcoming Families started, together with Caritas, AVSI, and other organizations, a place of help, hospitality, and support for refugees.

On May 18, 2022, for the fortieth anniversary of the Association, there was a pilgrimage to visit the Pope. The Holy Father greeted the families present in Saint Peter's Square with his blessing: "Persevere in faith and in the culture of hospitality."

At the Rimini Meeting in 2022, Welcoming Families promoted the exhibit "Not *how*, but *that*. The surprise of gratuitousness." The fullness experienced in the practice of hospitality can touch the heart of anyone we encounter. It is the challenge that was proposed to a group of artists for the Meeting: to visit, to encounter families, and to express, in their own artistic form, what they had seen; the *that* which had struck them through the *how*.

From the exhibit was born this initiative: fourteen artists took part, and their works told of the encounter they had had, opening to all those who visited the exhibit the possibility of becoming protagonists. "With their human and artistic sensibility, they well represented the surprise that arises from running into people who are absolutely normal," stresses Luca Sommacal, President of Welcoming Families, "who through simple gestures of welcome indicate a road that is possible for everyone."

Useful information

The headquarters of the Welcoming Families Association is in Milan:
Via Macedonio Melloni 27, 27 -20129 Milan, Italy.
Telephone: +39 02-70006152
Fax: +39 02-70006156
Email: *segreteria.nazionale@famiglieperaccoglienza.it*

Textual Sources

"The Reason for Charity": Contribution of Msgr. Luigi Giussani entitled *Fondamenti antropologici e metologici della condivisione* [Anthropological and methodological foundations of sharing] in *Accoglienza, volto del gratuito* [Welcoming, the face of gratuitousness], Act of the Conference of the Famiglie per l'Accoglienza Association, Milan, June 8, 1985, EDIT Editoriale Italiana, Milan 1985, pp. 1-9.

"Living Gratuitousness": Notes from the Beginning Day for the adults of Communion and Liberation in the Diocese of Milan, October 2, 1988.

"A New Experience of Humanity": Meeting with the Famiglie per l'Accoglienza, October 2, 1988. The meeting took place the same afternoon as the Beginning Day mentioned in the previous chapter.

"Not of Flesh, Nor of Blood, but of God Are We Born": Notes from a conversation of Luigi Giussani with the leadership of the Famiglie per l'Accoglienza, June 4, 1989. The title is taken from John 1:13.

"Embracing What is Different": Notes from a conversation of Luigi Giussani with the National Board of the Famiglie per l'Accoglienza Association, Milan, June 22, 1991.

"The Imitation of Christ": Notes from a conversation of Luigi Giussani with the National Board of Famiglie per l'Accoglienza, Milan, November 7, 1992.

"Familiarity as the Method of the Mystery": Meeting of Luigi Giussani with the National Board of the Famiglie per l'Accoglienza, January 28, 1996. Originally published in *Guardare all'origine*, manuscript edited by the Famiglie per l'Accoglienza, Milan 1996, pp. 7-14.

"The Person, Subject of a Relationship": Notes from a conversation with Luigi Giussani on the family, Milan, 1972.

"Culture of Life and Culture of Death": Intervention of Luigi Giussani at the International Theological-Pastoral Congress on "Children, springtime of the family and of society." Organized by the Pontifical Council for the Family on the occasion of the Jubilee of the Family (Rome, October 10-12, 2000).

Notes

1 Jean-Paul Sartre, *La Nausée*, Paris, Editions Gallimard, 1938, translation ours.

2 Benedict XVI, *Meeting with Young Couples*, Ancona, September 11, 2011.

3 Literally, "Families for Welcome," which henceforward we will translate as "Welcoming Families." www.famiglieperaccoglienza.it.

4 See below, "Familiarity as the Method of the Mystery."

5 See below, "The Reason for Charity."

6 Benedict XVI, *Meeting with Young Couples*, Ancona, September 11, 2011.

7 See below, "The Reason for Charity."

8 Luigi Giussani, *L'attrattiva Gesù*, BUR, Milan, 1999, 204, translation ours.

9 Angelo Scola, *Lettera alla Diocesi*, September 14, 2011, translation ours.

10 See below, "Familiarity as the Method of the Mystery."

11 Editor's note: The English words that correspond to the Italian word *gratuità* (a free, spontaneous act of giving) all pose difficulties: "gratuity" can sound like giving someone a tip and "the gratuitous" conjures up gratuitous sex and violence in contemporary culture. We have chosen the somewhat ponderous "gratuitousness" as the best option available.

12 Editor's note: The word Fr. Giussani uses here, *condiscendenza*, presents a challenge to the translator. The word is similar to "condescension"—but rather than the usual English connotation of a smug, superior attitude, it means something closer to God's gracious descent to shape himself to our limited understanding. We have chosen another word theologians have traditionally used for this concept: "accommodation."

13 Pope Saint John Paul II.

14 C.M. Martini, *Itinerari Educativi*, Second Letter for the pastoral program "Educare," Centro Ambrosiano di Documentazione e Studi Religiosi, Milan, 1988.

15 Beginning Day is the assembly of the Communion and Liberation movement that marks the beginning of the social year, offering guidelines for the journey that the community will make in that year.

16 Vladimir Soloviev, *A Short Story of the Antichrist*.

17 Ibid.

18 Reference to the ecclesial movement Communion and Liberation (CL), founded by Fr. Luigi Giussani in 1954. It began in the city of Milan and then rapidly diffused throughout all of Italy and is now present in about ninety countries on every continent.

19 John Paul II, *Redemptor Hominis*, March 4, 1979.

20 C.M. Martini, *Itinerari educativi*, 28.

21 C. Pavese, *Il metiere di vivere*, Einaudi, Turin, 1952, 191.

22 The Compagnia delle Opere (Company of Works) is a non-profit organization founded on July 11, 1986. It arose from graduates and young adults, both in CL and not, as a witness to a particular education and a mature faith. The organization aims to promote and protect the "dignified presence within people in a social context and of everyone, as well as the presence of works and companies in society, encouraging a conception of the market and its rules as understanding and respecting the person in all the aspects, dimensions, and moments of life."

23 *Litterae Communionis* refers to the magazine of Communion and Liberation, now called *Traces*.

24 *Rose e il lebbroso* [Rose and the Leper], in *Litterae Communionis* n.11 (November 1988), 6-7. Here is an excerpt from the letter: "While I was coming back from helping Eugenia, I passed through the clinic when I saw what looked like a corpse under the table. I bent down while a nurse told me, 'Leave him alone. He is a man who walks on four legs. Look at his stumps and his feet!' It was already night. The leper had left at seven that morning and had traveled three hours to cover the kilometer that separated him from the hospital. He had dysentery and had asked to be treated. He had already been refused the admission form because he could not pay the fee. He was weak and depressed and told me, 'Could I die now? What sense is there in me living?' I did not have any money to help him, but I took a prescription pad from a nurse, put the leper on a wheelchair, and went to the on-call doctor. The doctor first yelled at me, then asked me, 'What's wrong with the old man? Is he your relative?' So, I told him, and the doctor asked if I was a nun. I answered, 'No, but I am a Catholic Christian.' I wanted to have the companionship of the movement near me because I did not know what to do with the old leper. Even my nurse friends mocked me instead of helping me. I went to the kitchen to ask for food for the man, and they responded that if I wanted to give him food, I would have to give up my

dinner. I was very hungry, and I did not feel like fasting, but there was no other way. I gave my plate to the leper who was very hungry. The nurses asked me, 'You're letting him use your plate?' 'Of course,' I responded. I brought the sick man to the corner of a room, gave him my blanket and my pullover, and he fell asleep in peace. In the morning I met the doctor who was on his way to visit the leper. He said, 'Pray for me.'"

25 The Meeting is an annual event, launched in 1980, which emerged out of the experience of Communion and Liberation. Held in the city of Rimini, its full name is "The Meeting for the Friendship Amongst Peoples." It features speakers, panels, and exhibitions on a wide range of topics.

26 *Il Sabato* was a Catholic periodical in Italy from 1978 to 1993.

27 "Il criterio non è mai politico," in *Litterae Communionis* n.11 (November 1988), 6.

28 "Oh Come, Creator Spirit Come," trans. Robert Seymour Bridges (1899).

29 In this regard, see Luigi Giussani, *The Work of the Movement: The Fraternity of Communion and Liberation*, Cooperativa Nuovo Mondo, 2005.

30 The ecclesial association *Memores Domini* is a group of CL members who have chosen to live their dedication to Christ and to the Church in virginity. The association was recognized by the Holy See in 1988.

31 The Union of Families is an association that came out of Milan in 1982 and is now spread throughout Italy with over fifty thousand families registered. The association proposes itself as a protection for families defending and promoting the family on the cultural, social, political, and economic levels. Like the Welcoming Families Association, it is part of the *Forum of Family Associations* constituted at Rome at the request of the Italian Bishops Conference.

32 The Movimento Populare (MP) was born in Milan in 1975. Some adults who had been formed in Communion and Liberation and other Catholics gave life to an instrument that favors a Christian presence in Italian society, following the tradition of Catholic political movements and following the directives of the bishops. Following the birth and the development of the Companionship of Works, which assumed the ideal and the heritage of the MP, it ceased its activities in 1993.

33 The magazine of Communion and Liberation, now called *Traces*.

34 Ada Negri, *My Youth*, translated by Maria A. Costantini.

35 From an Italian proverb: "*Chi fa falla*": "Those who act make mistakes."

36 Luigi Giussani, *The Religious Sense*, McGill Queen's University Press, 1997, 100ff.

37 John Paul II, *Dives in Misericordia*, December 2, 1980.

38 O.V. Milosz, *Miguel Mañara*, Jaca Book, Milan, 2001, 68. Translation ours.

39 Starting in 1958, a few hundred students in Gioventù Studentesca (Student Youth) from Milan began to gather every week in the Bassa, south of Milan. For a few hours, they accompanied young people in the farms dispersed throughout the countryside, alternating times of play with moments of reading and catechesis, together with parishes in the area. Thus "charitable work" was born, which now constitutes one of the fundamental gestures of the educational proposal of Communion and Liberation. Today, thousands of people, in Italy and in the world, learn that the law of existence is gratuitousness, the imitation of Jesus of Nazareth. People who are thus educated tend to live this law in every circumstance of their life, to the point of generating works like the sharing of needs and seeking answers to make society better. Cf. Luigi Giussani, "The Meaning of Charitable Work."

40 Cf. Luigi Giussani, *The Religious Sense*.

41 The Assemblies of Leaders were periodic gatherings held by Father Giussani for the leaders of the Italian and foreign communities of Communion and Liberation.

42 Luigi Giussani, *Why the Church?*, McGill Queen's University Press, 2001.

43 Heraclitus, *Fragments*, Fragment 54.

44 Taking up this invitation, starting the next October (1997), the Association, in its various local chapters, has always started the social year with a pilgrimage to a Marian shrine or to the tomb of Saint Riccardo Pampuri.

45 Dionysius the Areopagite, *De Divinis Nominibus*, 953 A 10.

46 Gioventù Studentesca, or "GS": high school students who follow the charism of Communion and Liberation.

47 Saint Ambrose, *Hexameron*, IX, 76.

48 Luigi Giussani, *Alla ricerca del volto umano*, Rizzoli, Milan, 1995.

49 Declaration on Christian Education, *Gravissimum educationis*, October 28, 1965.

50 John Paul II, *Evangelium vitae*, 7.

51 *Evangelium vitae*, 1.

52 *Evangelium vitae*, 80.

53 "You have given to the conjugal community the sweet law of love and the indissoluble bond of peace, so that the chaste and fruitful union of the spouses may increase the number of your children. With this admirable design you, O Father, have allowed that the birth of new creatures gladden the human family and their rebirth in Christ build up your Church." Preface of the Liturgy of Matrimony, Ambrosian Rite.

54 *Evangelium vitae*, 92.

55 G. Bassani, trans. William Weaver. Everyman's Library, 2011.

56 *Evangelium vitae*, 79.

57 *Evangelium vitae*, 101.

58 *Evangelium vitae*, 29.

59 John Paul II, *Address to the Italian National Congress of the Ecclesial Movement for Cultural Commitment*, 2 (16 January 1982).

60 Later Patriarch of Venice and Archbishop of Milan, a long-time supporter of the work of Welcoming Families Association.

61 By foster care is meant the temporary insertion in a new family of a child in difficulty in its own family, because of various problems with the child's natural parents.

62 Luigi Giussani, Letter of June 2002, on the occasion of the Association's twentieth anniversary.

This book was set in Adobe Caslon Pro, designed by Carol Twombly and released in 1990. The typeface is named after the British typefounder William Caslon (1692-1766) and grew out of Twombly's study of Caslon's specimen sheets. Though Caslon began his career making "exotic" typefaces—Hebrew, Arabic, and Coptic—his Roman typeface became the standard for text printed in English for most of the eighteenth century, including the Declaration of Independence.

This book was designed by Shannon Carter, Ian Creeger, and Gregory Wolfe. It was published in hardcover, paperback, and electronic formats by Slant Books, Seattle, Washington.

Cover art: Beatriz Zerolo, "Origins," 150 x 150 cm. Oil, pigments, and rope on linen.